THE LONG CROSSING

The Long Crossing

First Printing: 2017

ISBN 978-0-692-44556-3

H&H Publications
PO 937
206 East Grand River
Fowlerville, MI 48836

Cover design by Vonette Bigham
Book design by Lisa Tomczyk
Editing assistance by Mell Coleman

THE LONG CROSSING

Selected Writings by Steve Horton 1975-2014

Published by

H&H PUBLICATIONS

To Dawn,
There at the start of each new day

The Kids and Grandkids
&
Other Family Members and Friends
- Past & Present -

Orange streaks over the foggy eastern shore,

pierces through this soft parade of summer smoke…

in the distance was the light of home.

Steve Horton (Written in San Francisco during the fall of 1972)

Keep true to the dreams of thy youth…
Found on the writing desk of
novelist Herman Millville after his death

Table of Contents

A Foreward 8
From the Front Porch 11
In the North Country 19
Memorial Day: Then & Now 23
Notes on the Bird Season 25
Recalling the '68 Campaign 28
This River Never Forgets 32
Life in the Detroit Lions Press Box 35
The DJ Returns 37
At the End of a Fishing Trip 39
A Country Christmas 41
A Trip on the Platte River 44
Golden Slumbers & the 60's 45
The Hunter Does Not Always Hunt 47
Kennedy and Us 49
On Getting Married 52
Horton Bay & Hemingway 54
A Child Is Born 57
A Reunion at a Place Called 'Memories' 59
Pondering the Camping Life 61
Kicking Up Some Dust 64
The "New" Electric Pencil Sharpener Arrives 67
Local Participation Key to Self-Government 69
Christmas Returns 71
Frankenmuth Visited: Family Fun Center 73
Wide Awake & Thinking 76
A Mouse and a Cat…In the House 79

On Writing **81**
An Ordinary Fishing Story **84**
Lessons in Art **88**
Echoes from Past Novembers **100**
At the Straits of Mackinac **111**
The Morning Rain **113**
On Sinatra & Song **115**
This Business of Horses **118**
At the End of a Fair Week **121**
Visiting the Gerald R. Ford Presidential Museum **124**
A Walk in the Park **128**
At the Campfire **134**
Tears for a Departed Friend **136**
On Progress **139**
Winter: A Harsh Beauty **143**
A Trail Ride **145**
On This Cool Autumn Morning **150**
The End of a 4-H Career **153**
Graduation Day: A Time of Hopes and Dreams **155**
Deer Hunting **158**
The Harsh Word **160**
Mackinac Bridge: Connecting Michigan **163**
Indian Summer at Michigan State **166**
A Memory That Keeps Me Warm **172**
Tom Braun: A Man with Heart **175**
A Christmas Carol: Still Relevant **180**
Pure Michigan on Hall Lake **186**
Facing 'Hard Stuff': Coleman Young's Story Offers Lesson **189**
The Long Crossing **195**

A Foreward

It was Christmas morning in 1963, my seventh-grade year in school and a few weeks after President Kennedy had been assassinated. As we were taking turns opening our presents, my father handed me a wrapped box. Inside the box was a small portable typewriter. Elated at this unexpected gift, I soon began making plans to publish a newspaper. By necessity, the stories (in my first and only edition) were limited to one side of an 8.5 x 11 inch sheet of paper, and I only produced a couple of copies. My typing skills were non-existent, and the convenience of a copy machine loomed far off in the future. The memory is foggy, but I'm guessing I must have indicated to my mother a desire to become a writer or produce a newspaper. If so, then this dual aspiration dates back to early youth.

During that same transitional year I enjoyed what I thought was a serious relationship with a young lady, a fellow classmate. Other boys, in similar commitments, had purchased an inexpensive ring and given this token of affection to their respective girlfriends. I followed suit; however a day later my beloved returned the ring. Needless to say, the romance quickly withered; I could see that her interest had wandered elsewhere.

In any case the pattern was set. Writing, newspapers, and girls would occupy much of my attention in the ensuing years. I had other interests and aspirations, but those prevailed. I've been a working newspaperman for nearly 40 years, starting with a short-lived weekly called *The New Review* that I helped with in the late summer and fall of 1975. The following year I secured a job as a stringer with the *Livingston County Press* and its sister publication *The Fowlerville Review*. A landmark event occurred as a result of that latter employment. In June of 1976, shortly after starting, I received my first paycheck as a reporter. Prior to that compensation, my efforts at the writing desk were sporadic, less-than-successful, and failed to create any income.

As for the fairer sex, that interest led to marriage and from that union I gained two step-daughters, a son, and then grandchildren. School trips, 4-H activities, the fair, band concerts, assorted pets, and Walt Disney animated features became topics of newspaper columns.

The bulk of my career has been spent publishing the *Fowlerville News & Views*, a weekly newspaper that my wife Dawn and I started in January of 1985, a few weeks before our wedding date.

I've tackled all kinds of news stories over the years, the subject matter ranging from reports on village council meetings and political campaigns to sports contests and community celebrations. I've penned dozens of profiles, eulogies, meeting announcements, and historical retrospectives. Were I to compile all of those accounts, large and small, and place them between the covers of a book, I believe the result would make *War and Peace* look like a short story. Even so, unless someone had an interest in local history or the minutia of small-town affairs, most of the contents would hold little interest to the average reader.

My output has included other writings: informal essays that contained personal observations and reminiscences along with commentaries on social and political issues. And every now and then I threw in a fishing story. I've put together a cross section of these works for this book, beginning with those written early in my career to more recent compositions. With many of these offerings I had an ulterior motive; I wished to champion a point of view or to be instructive. In other selections I simply sought to offer a slice-of-life. In all of them I wanted to be creative in both style and presentation and to test myself as a writer. Last but not least, I wrote them because I hoped to engage the reader.

These writings span a 40-year period and cover a wide range of subject matter and themes, yet as I went over them for editing purposes, I discovered a tendency to re-visit familiar territory. Certain themes, settings, reflections, historical details, and analogies, used in earlier pieces, have shown up in later works. I suppose that's not unusual for a writer. I've noticed its occurrence when reading the collected works of other scribes. In my case it's the consequence of bringing all of these disparate columns, done as stand-alone pieces and separated by a number of years, and putting them under one roof.

I started out with the goal of having 40 selections for this edition. However, as I got into the compilation, recalling different columns I'd done in the past, the number gradually expanded. The list was in danger of growing even longer when, fearing I'd become an overindulgent father, I said "that's it" after typing still another of my golden oldies. The rest of my offspring will remain (for the time being) in the pile of old newspapers, or kept in the anonymity of a computer file.

These selected writings are, first and foremost, favorites of mine. But my criteria also included picking ones that I felt would be enjoyable for the reader and possessed a whiff of durability and longevity.

As a boy, I dreamed of writing stories, publishing newspapers, and falling in love with a pretty girl. I imagined other possibilities, too, but those three came true and are still being pursued. The journey has not been smooth and "steady as she goes." Along the way there have been choppy seas, difficult straits, ill-advised choices, obstacles, re-assessments, and changes in direction. The roughest passages have, of course, been the loss of loved ones.

Still, despite a few bumps, bruises and heartache I'm a lucky fellow. Fortune has been kind to me. I've been blessed with family and friends, past and present, and with a career that's given me a livelihood and much satisfaction. But looking forward is still the better view. Among my ambitions, held since boyhood, was to publish a book of my writings. After a long crossing, here it is.

November 16, 2014

From the Front Porch

THE TWILIGHT HOUR. I sit on the front porch of our new residence, a large Victorian-style, burgundy-colored house, located a block off downtown Fowlerville. We moved into the place at the end of April with the intention of having the newspaper office in the front two rooms and living in the rest. In a manner of speaking, we now live over the store.

The problem with moving, whether it's a household or office, is that most of us have more possessions than we need. And when you're downsizing your space, as we did, you find yourself with much more stuff than you have room. So we did a lot of packing, a lot of deciding what to keep and what to get rid of and then a lot of unpacking and sorting out. For most of the summer, we've been slowly settling in.

This place was built by a pair of brothers in 1898. They worked as carpenters and other homes that they constructed, similar in appearance, can be found elsewhere in town. The legacy of their craft lives on.

For the past 30 years, up until we pulled into town with a packed U-Haul truck and several other accompanying vehicles filled to the brim, I've called Hastings "home." But for 28 of those years my wife and I have owned and operated the *Fowlerville News & Views*, so we've been commuters, driving back-and-forth three or four times a week. A lot of miles traveled, a lot of hours spent inside a car. One of the motivations for relocating here (besides combining the home and office and thus cutting that extra expense) was to end the commute.

In the early evening, instead of driving along the highway, I now have time to sit on the front porch and watch the daylight ebb and the shadows lengthen.

But while I've acclimated myself to this new home, the disruption of routine and pattern initially put me in a funk, had me feeling a bit melancholy, gloomy and out-of-sorts. I still attended to the duties of journalism, producing the news stories and profiles and putting out the weekly editions. But I was unable to motivate myself to return to the writing desk and create the personal essays and social commentaries. I'd stopped doing them a month or so before the move, needing all the free time I had to both pack and discard. However, after arriving here, despite a couple of halfhearted attempts, nothing has been produced. Staying away, avoiding the task, became easier and easier.

My old saboteur was whispering in my ear again. My dark mood had emboldened him to crawl out of the mental recesses. "What difference does it make what you write?" he asked. "What's the point? Who cares what you have to say?"

In the past I have always answered him, "But what if it does make a difference? What if there is a point?" And I would continue with these questions directed at him, "If I don't try, then who should do so in my place? Do I make excuses and remain on the sideline or join those who are in the arena?"

Back and forth the debate would go— to write or not to write— until finally, tired of the inactivity, I'd sit down, start off with one true sentence and, in doing so, I'd return to the arena.

About a mile to the northeast of this front porch, as the crow flies, sets a small, white clapboard house on Sharp Road. It was here that my father and mother, Verlyn and June, brought me, their firstborn, from the Howell Hospital. Fourteen months later my sister Carol arrived. They had rented this place from my father's grandparents (my great-grandparents), Rollin and Blanche Horton, who had inherited it from Blanche's uncle, William Durfee. The house and 40 acres were what remained of a larger farm that belonged to her grandparents, Emory and Cordelia Durfee.

An austere beginning, my mother would later recall. Uncle Bill's place featured an outdoor privy and no indoor plumbing except for a hand pump in the kitchen. Mom would remark about the challenges of having two babies without the convenience of that plumbing. Shortly afterwards we moved to a farm on Finlan Road, owned by an uncle and aunt (George and Thelma) that did offer this amenity. My folks worked the farm on shares, milking cows, raising a few hogs, and growing the traditional crops of hay, oats, corn, and wheat.

We re-located to still another farm on North Fowlerville Road when George and Thelma sold the property on Finlan Road and purchased this place. We were living there when my brother, Craig, arrived. A couple of years later we moved again, this time to the farm on North Gregory Road. It was owned by my grandparents, Lloyd and Illah Mae Horton. This is where I grew up; the place I consider *home*.

After my father died (when I was 16), we remained for several months. My mother, who did not relish farm life, had focused her energies and hopes on building a small ranch-style house in a subdivision near town. Once finished this place became our new home. I continued working for my grandfather until leaving for college.

Mom would eventually depart for Lansing, wishing to be closer to where she worked (the East Lansing office of United Parcel Service). She would get married, come back to Fowlerville, retire due to her illness, and then locate in Potterville where she lived until her death. I, meanwhile, would reside in East Lansing, San Francisco (briefly), Lansing, Perry, Traverse City, Williamston, Fowlerville again, and then Hastings. And now back again in Fowlerville.

You could say I've come nearly full circle from that house on Sharp Road to this front porch. In geographical terms I haven't made it too far. But travel involves more than physical movement. During the course of one's life, there are journeys of the mind and of the heart that take us many places and create a potpourri of experiences. We work, raise families, enjoy our triumphs, suffer our sorrows, and grow older. If we're lucky, the accumulation and combination of those assorted travels will result in a depth and breadth of character and perhaps a little wisdom.

If that crow were to veer off a little to the right in its flight from the porch to my first home, it would fly over Greenwood Cemetery. Among the things I do, three or four times a week, is go on a long walk. I have different routes, including one that takes me east on Grand River, past the post office, and then into this cemetery. Using the circular drive, I go past the graves of my grandparents, a few aunts and uncles, and then over to the back end where my mother's remains are buried. From there I head towards the old part of Greenwood and walk past the plots of my father and sister who lay side-by-side; he died at age 38 and she at age 21. Next to them on one side are the graves of Rollin and Blanche Horton and William Durfee, while on the other side rest the remains of Rollin's parents, Stephen and Elizabeth, and his sister Alta Minkley.

It is a familiar setting— not one I am apprehensive about. Blanche (whom our family called 'Mammy') liked coming here and tending to the grave sites of family members. She and Grandpa Rollin were in their 80's when I was a young boy, and I often stayed with them. When I accompanied them to this cemetery, I'd help Grandpa carry the pails as he watered the flowers and plants while Mammy pulled weeds.

Across the driveway from the Horton plots are the grave markers of her beloved grandparents, Emory and Cordelia, her baby son, Wilfred who died at six months of age, her aunts, Anna and Edith, and her mother, Helen. Her father, George Huck, had died of diphtheria before she was born, catching it from his two-year-old son who also died from the disease. Her mother went to Lansing to work as a seamstress and then later married Eugene Cheney, a widower.

Mammy grew up in her grandparents' home, located at the corner of Sharp and Hogback Roads. The Durfees had purchased the land in 1866, moving here from Livonia where they had a farm. Both had come originally from western New York. They had nine children—four daughters and five sons. The first seven were born on the Wayne County farm and the two youngest on the Sharp Road homestead. The youngest, Anna, died first, just shy of her 36th birthday. She was followed four months later by her father, Emory. Edith was a school teacher, while Alfred migrated to Colorado where he would be elected to the state House and then the state Senate. William was a farmer.

Her uncle, Stephen Durfee, was the one she held up as a role model for me. Seeing my love of reading and seeking to encourage me, Mammy would tell how he'd be plowing a field with a team of horses and, needing to rest them, would find a shade tree and use the opportunity to read a book. He went on to become a school teacher, a school commissioner and when he moved to Port Arthur, Texas, a custom inspector.

I'm sure as Stephen Durfee and his family prepared to leave, they had to make decisions on what to keep and what to leave behind, just as we did with our recent move. Among the items that didn't make the trip was a trunk full of books. Mammy kept the trunk, storing it in her attic and, as a boy exploring that exotic space in their household, I discovered its contents. Inside the cover of each book was a label stating, "Private Library of Stephen Durfee." When Mammy passed away in 1975, followed a few months later by Grandpa Rollin (I had turned 24 that year), her instructions were that I be given these books.

Since then I've taken them with me on my various re-locations. A number of them are not really anything special and will probably end up getting discarded one day, but others I think are worth holding onto and passing on, including several volumes of the *History of England* by Thomas Macaulay, a book of essays by Ralph Waldo Emerson, several of George Eliot's novels, books about the Spanish American War, a volume detailing the hurricane that devastated Galveston, Texas, and several texts dealing with American history. Interestingly, the Spanish-American War and Galveston Hurricane occurred about the same time this house I now live in was built—1898.

I haven't read all of the books in the Stephen Durfee Library, and it's unlikely I'll ever find the time or interest to do so. Too many other pressing priorities. Still, they are treasured keepsakes; physical links from one generation to another. A reminder of how my great-grandmother sought to instruct and inspire me. And did so. And still does; her influence lingers on.

Now I walk past the tombstones of the Durfees these many years later. The names and dates have become weathered, covered by green mold, and barely discernible. The words on the Horton markers, while newer, also show the erosion brought on by nature and the passing years. I wonder, after I and the other family members of my generation are gone, if anyone will remember who they were. Will a boy or girl not yet born— who can trace their lineage back to these people— visit this spot one day, decorate it with flowers, and in some manner bring back the memory of their lives?

Yet I know that a future date will come when they will be forgotten, as I will. The memories of us, like a dwindling fire, will slowly but surely dissipate until, like a dying ember, the last glow is gone. Maybe all that will eventually remain of who we were will be our name on a family tree, put there by a future genealogist. Perhaps, if fortune is kind, there'll be a short biography, containing as much information as research can glean. So, with that possibility in mind, I put these words on paper in hopes that one day they might be found and read; that they might re-kindle the memories of those family members I loved, evoking their names and lives once more. And not only them, but also those ancestors I did not know, ones whose graves I now walk past, wondering about them, what they were like and what kind of lives they lived.

Among the boxes we hauled over from Hastings to this new home was one containing some of my personal mementos. It included old articles I'd written when first starting out, research papers from high school and college, old photos of myself and friends, and a few magazines and newspapers with articles I felt important enough to keep. From time to time in the past, I've gone through the contents whenever I felt like taking a trip down memory lane.

As I was getting ready to find a place to store this box in our new abode, I decided to look at the items once again. Along with the many familiar items was an 11-by-17 inch envelope, stuffed full. I couldn't recall what was inside, so I opened it and pulled out the contents. Like an archeologist discovering a long-buried treasure, I found letters, notes, greeting cards, and photos that spanned a time frame from 1969 to 1979. I realized that I hadn't read any of this correspondence or seen the pictures in perhaps 20 years. In fact, there were many of the items I'd forgotten that I even had.

The photos (wallet size black and whites) were graduation pictures of several of my Fowlerville High classmates, with messages written on the back. One girl said I was the best-looking guy in class. I'd always thought so, too, but then I suspect she might have said the same to other boys. Several wished me "good luck in the future" and predicted I'd accomplish much. I hope I have and will continue to do so. "Cool" was a favorite word back in 1969, and many of the classmates told me I was a "cool guy." Being "cool" and accepted by your peers when you're young (or even when you're older) is a desired goal.

There were poignant letters; one from my mother, sent after I'd moved away to Michigan State, saying how much she missed having me living at home, adding that she understood that this was part of life. "But," she added, "I still miss you."

Another, in shaky handwriting, came from my sister when she was a patient at Henry Ford Hospital. She said that her illness had caused her to lose a lot of weight, which she thought was good, and that she and her fiancé would visit me in Traverse City in the fall. That visit never occurred. She would pass away from her illness within a few weeks. Still another note had been written by the desk clerk at the hotel where I stayed in that northern city, slid under the door of the room I rented, telling me, "Your great-grandfather has died."

And there were several letters I came across; one from a friend I had in college; another from a co-worker who I'd worked with at Big Boy the first year I was in Traverse City; and others from a couple of fellow reporters whom I knew from my days at the *Livingston County Press*. I also came across birthday greetings and postcards as well as a farewell card signed by the staff at the *Press* when I left for what I thought would be greener pastures.

Reading several of the letters and cards brought back warm memories. I felt this overpowering urge to reach back and somehow re-connect with those who'd once been close. I wondered why we had allowed ourselves to drift so far from each other. Yet drift apart we did. The passing years, changing circumstances, different directions, and personal choices had widened the space more and more until each of us has gone over our respective horizon. And while we might wonder how the other has fared and, once in awhile we are able to re-connect with one of them, the hard fact is that most are gone forever.

While I'd forgotten much of what was in that envelope, I came across a pair of letters that I remembered quite well. I'd wondered what had happened to them, not imagining that I would have thrown them away. Grandma Horton mailed them to me shortly after I'd quit college. She expressed her concern about my decision to leave Michigan State, but more so she worried about the direction I seemed to be taking and other choices I'd made.

I wanted to be a writer. I even considered myself one. But I didn't have any clear blueprint on how to accomplish this career goal or how to make it a paying proposition. I'd taken a couple of stabs at trying to get hired at a newspaper. However, even I realized that I lacked any journalistic credentials or on-the-job training that would impress an editor. I was mainly wishing and hoping.

In her letters, Grandma told me the importance of safeguarding one's health. "Good health is one of the most important possessions we have," she said. My grandmother, as usual, was right, but like many young men I was prone to burn the candle at both ends, not realizing I needed a little wax left for later years. And I read again her counsel on self-esteem, a passage that I well recalled. In her letters, Grandma explained that this personal attribute was not to be confused with self-importance or arrogance or an over-inflated ego, but she added that "each of us needs to realize and accept that we are worthy and have value and a part of gaining this self-confidence is avoiding self-destructive habits and behavior."

I remember feeling a little uncomfortable about this self-esteem message. I had the uneasy sense that she could see past the youthful bravado and discern the saboteur lurking in the shadows; see the doubt, uncertainty and insecurity that this dark nemesis fed off and helped perpetuate. We exchanged letters, but I kept this portion of her message at arm's length. My grandmother's other intent with these letters, as well as with other actions, was to do all that she could to keep me from becoming estranged from my family and from drifting away. I can say that she employed all of the tricks in her grandmotherly bag.

While I did not heed all of her good advice— in some ways I needed to fend for myself, suffer a few goose eggs and skinned knees, and figure things out for myself— the ties of family were not severed, and eventually a wife, son, step-daughters, grandchildren, and in-laws were added to the family tree.

Her words, written on a page, are as powerful now as they were then. Like the other keepsakes I discovered in the envelope, they are heralds from the past. Her letters are reminders of love and caring that reach across the long span and even the boundary of death. Their impact continues.

Reading all of this correspondence again was like pulling the curtains open and letting in the bright light. I had brooded long enough in the gloomy room. I needed to take a broom to the cobwebs and soap and water to the dusty floor. I needed once again to push the saboteur back into the mental recesses and return to the writing table. While putting out a newspaper each week remains an essential task, both because it is my stock-in-trade and because it financially keeps the wolf from the door, and while I take satisfaction in reporting the governmental news, doing the profiles of local people, and helping promote the various special events, I find an inner satisfaction in crafting the personal essays and commentaries on public affairs. These forms of composition and expression help bolster my self-esteem; they are a key part of what I bring to the arena, and they allow me to offer ideas and thoughts that I hope make a difference.

Still, I do not regret listening to the doubter again nor do I regard this most recent lapse into inactivity as time ill spent. I have come to realize that the gloomy mood is part of my make-up, part of what makes me tick. It brings a little sour to the sweetness and, for me, this combination makes life tastier.

I write what I write with conviction and with all of the tools of persuasion I can muster. I do so with confidence. Yet perversely, the doubt and uncertainty help keep me (or so I hope) from sounding self-important, from thinking my opinions are infallible, and from believing my words ought to be chiseled in stone. "Don't take yourself so seriously," an older friend once advised me, "no one else does." I always thought that a good caution.

From the front porch of this new home, here in the twilight hour, the words from an old Sinatra song come back; a song about the cycles of living and the rough spots. The words remind me that even when you're feeling down and out, even when the doubts appear and then linger, you keep going and see what tomorrow has in store.

"I've been told, and I believe, that life is meant for living" is how the lyric goes. I find the sentiment encouraging. So I move on. Back home once more, nearly full circle from where I started, yet between then and now I've seen a few places and done a few things. Perhaps the experiences gained—and any lessons learned—would be worth sharing. Something left for giving even as the moments are getting fewer. And so I give them, these words, to you.

In the North Country

Then there were the fishermen. Early each morning they'd steer their small boats slowly across the waters of the Bay. Their lines trailed off behind, weighed down with heavy sinkers.

The seagulls would make wide circles above them and beyond, fingering out into the middle of the waters, was the dark green and brown of the peninsula.

You could watch them from the restaurant. Always after the waitress brought the coffee and as you let it cool. It was quiet then.

Later, outside, the air would be cool and fresh. A slight breeze was often blowing in off the Bay. Along Front Street, the washed-over pavement glistened from the reflected sun.

I'd walk slowly back along it, pass the closed stores, to the room where I stayed.

* * *

That July afternoon we drove into Honor. We slowed down as we passed through the town and then at the outskirts stopped at Bud's Sporting Goods. The attendant, a middle-aged man, came out.

"Afternoon," he nodded.

"How's it going?" asked Zdan. "The trout fishing any good?"

"Not sure," the man hesitated. "I heard they've been catching some browns over by the swamp."

"You're talking about the Platte?" I asked.

He nodded and then added, "The part of the river just above the lake."

"How about the Betsie?" I wondered.

"He shook his head. "Water's too warm."

We asked a few more questions, mostly to make conversation, then thanked him and drove off. A short distance away we turned from the highway onto a dirt road that led through the swamp. We followed it until we reached a bridge that crossed the Platte.

The river was shallow here, and its course twisting. The current flowed quick and rough in spots, splashing white-foamed over the stumps and fallen trees.

We took out our poles and stepped carefully into the water. Slowly we edged downstream.

I moved out ahead and started casting over the small, protected pools near the bank and behind the logs as well as out into the middle of the swift current. Zdan trailed behind, working those stretches in a similar fashion, only using different bait.

I went along for several hundred yards, going past two wide bends. Finally, just before a third one, I spotted a large, still pool and headed over to it.

The sun was hot, and it glared brightly off parts of the surface. A thick growth of trees lined the banks, providing a bit of shade, their branches hanging green and heavy-looking. I cast the line out and then quickly began reeling it in. The lure was skimming along the surface when the trout struck it.

* * *

You could always watch the old men. They'd come each afternoon to fish off the Cass Street Dam. They'd stand in a row behind the steel railing, their lines pulled out into the tumbling waters that flowed through this man-made barricade. But just beyond this miniature waterfall, the Boardman River slowed to a more leisurely pace.

Each spring, when the suckers and steelheads made their runs, the trees beside the river would be bare and gnarled. But later on, as the pike arrived, they'd be adorned in their opulent green.

Late in the afternoon you could look down from the Union Street Bridge and see the fish resting. They'd quiver slightly, steadying themselves against the current. The riverbed was covered with small boulders, and downstream, along both banks, were broken-off dock pilings. Further on, past the pilings, the river began to horseshoe back through the town.

* * *

The tip of the pole bent sharply as I pulled the trout from the water. It was small and silver-specked.

Holding it tight, I pulled the hook from its mouth and gently put it back into the river.

"Just caught one," I yelled back to Zdan.

"How big?"

"Maybe seven inches," I answered.

"I haven't gotten any to bite yet," he called back. "I think I'll go back and try a spot that looks good."

"Check you later," I waved. Then I turned and headed downstream.

As I waded around another curve, the water swirled around my legs. The rush slowed a little as the river straightened out. A shallow sand-flat lay over to the right. Just beyond it was stand of marsh grass.

Casting over near the grass, I felt a tug. I worked the spot with several more tries without any success. Then a few yards out ahead, next to a fallen log, I felt the line pull hard. The trout jumped twice, breaking the surface as I reeled it in. But as I pulled it out, the pole bowing, I saw that I had another small one.

I let it go and moved further along. The warm afternoon wore on. The river had deepened past my waist and was no longer as fast flowing.

I had just begun to think of heading back when I felt another tug. The line jerked and then tightened. As I began to slowly edge the struggling fish towards me, I realized the pull was not a strong one. My suspicion was confirmed once the fish came out of the stream. Like the others, it was too small to keep.

"Three strikes and you're out," I thought as I let it go. Walking against the river's flow proved awkward and difficult. I stopped several times to rest before I reached the pool where I'd last seen Zdan fishing. I kept going and finally, as I rounded a bend, I spotted him sitting on the ground over near the bridge where we had parked the car, drinking a beer.

"Any luck?" I asked.

"No," he shook his head and took a sip from his can.

"How about yourself?"

"Just three runts, I said. "Nothing worth keeping."

I climbed out of the water and sat next to him. Zdan handed me a beer from the small cooler.

"That stuff's pretty rough walking in," I said, gesturing towards the river.

"You know it," he agreed.

"Well," I looked at him, "what river shall we try tomorrow?"

"I was thinking that we ought to try this one again," he said.

"Not here I hope."

"No. Over by the US-31 Bridge."

"Where we fished last year?"

"Yeah," he said.

"Sounds like a winner."

* * *

You could always walk about the city early in the evening. The houses were elegant with their Victorian facades and finely-trimmed lawns. The large trees would hang out over the sidewalks like canopies.

You could walk past the red neon motel signs that lined Front Street and then Munson Avenue.

Over along the shore, next to the marina, the green harbor light flashed out over the darkening waters. Out in the distance you could see the boats, silhouetted against the sky as they headed to port. The sun would set over the hills of Leelanau County; its final brilliant glow mirrored on the Bay's smooth surface.

Later, at The Parlor, the talk was subdued. The music sounded distant. The bartender would serve his drinks, while the waitresses moved discreetly about the faintly-lit room. You could sit alone and have your drink. There was always something to think about.

If you waited long enough and were very quiet, then the memories returned, echoing softly, filing past, a parade of ghosts. You could always turn though and look away. When you looked away, they could not haunt you.

Memorial Day: Then & Now

THEN... It was a tradition we had. The day America honored its fallen soldiers, marines, and sailors.

The 30th of each May, mid-morning, the parade would begin. From its starting point, the marchers would head through the downtown area towards the cemetery.

The sidewalks would be crowded; the people lined along each side watching the procession. The line-up included the color guard, the high school and junior high bands, the Gold and Blue Star Mothers, the women's auxiliaries, the boy and girl scout troops, the cub scouts and brownies, and, of course, the veterans.

The parade ended at the graveled drive that circled the cannon. Then the ceremony would begin with The National Anthem followed by prayers, a speech, the laying of the wreath, the firing of the rifles, and finally with the playing of *Taps*.

The holiday was first started in the northern states three years after the Civil War ended. On May 5, 1868, Commander-in-Chief John A. Logan of the Grand Army of the Republic (a fraternal organization of Union veterans) issued a general order designating May 30 "For the purposes of strewing with flowers or otherwise decorating the graves of comrades who died in defense of their country during the late rebellion." He did this "with the hope that it will be kept from year to year."

The idea caught on. It was quickly adopted in all the states and territories (except those that had fought with the Confederacy). Most people referred to it as Decoration Day. The center of attention soon became the members of the Grand Army of the Republic. They would attend church in a body on the Sunday prior to the holiday. Then on the 30th they would march *en mass*, led by the village band, to the local cemetery. There speeches were given, and music played.

The holiday was meant to be a solemn occasion. In 1878, the Commander of the GAR noted in the annual report "his regret that it was necessary to remind some of the comrades that the day is sacred to the memory of our heroic dead, and that it is not, in any sense, a time for pleasure excursions, or merry-making of any kind."

Time eventually would erode the ranks of the GAR. But the holiday continued with a younger generation of veterans replacing them in the parades. Then after World War I, the observance was changed to include the honoring of all those killed in action while serving the nation.

NOW... It has become a three-day holiday weekend, and the official start of the summer recreation season. We still have the parades and conduct the ceremonies. We still decorate the soldiers' graves. But that aspect of the holiday seems to have lost its emphasis amid the freeway traffic jams, the rush to northern campgrounds, the full schedule of athletic events, and the TV ad men peddling their various sales.

It began as a single day set aside to remember the losses of war. The fallen men whom John Logan referred to in 1868 as "...our heroic dead, who made their breasts a barricade. The cost of a free and undivided republic." He also said, "We should guard their graves with sacred vigilance."

(Written in May 1976)

Notes on the Bird Season

October 1976— On Opening Day we walk down the lane behind the barn. There is a cool, crisp smell to the air. Underfoot the grass rustles, dried and brittle after several frostings.

"Be ready, Dillingham warns me. "I've knocked a few roosters out of this fence row before."

I keep an eye out, but no birds flush. Then we reach the first swale and split apart. The undergrowth is thick, the field having laid fallow for several years. The grass is still damp from a rain that fell the day before. We move along, stopping every few yards, listening for a bird to cackle. We make several swipes back and forth and then rest and have a smoke.

"They're lying pretty tight," I say.

"Yeah," Dillingham replies. "They're probably holed up in that corn." He motions towards a nearby field.

"You'd need a dog to hunt it though," he adds.

I nod and mention his old hunting dog, Pooch. We both decide that we'd have better luck if old Pooch was still around. Though he lacked the refinements of the better-bred bird dogs, he could still flush out the pheasants. Whenever you hunted with him, you waited for his tail to start wagging and listened for a change in his bark. When he got a bird scent, you'd take off running behind him.

After talking about Pooch some more, we finish our smokes and head off across a newly-cut hayfield to another swale.

* * *

The following day. The rains from earlier in the week have turned into snow flurries. The sky to the west is a blackish blue. Cousin Ron Clark and his friend Eddie have been hunting the sticks and swales west of Uncle Bill's woods for most of the morning. I join them early in the afternoon.

"You wouldn't believe it," Ron tells me. "These birds are breaking cover a mile ahead of us. The dogs aren't even beginning to work them."

Ron and I walk along the windward side of a patch of sticks. Eddie takes the other side. A hen flushes, flying into the wind.

"Are you kidding me?" Ron jokes. "They're not supposed to do that."

We move further along. Another hen flushes a couple hundred feet ahead of us. Finally we reach the ditch and stop.

"There's got to be roosters around here some place," Ron says.

Eddie shakes his head. "This wind is keeping them in the corn."

After a minute or so we decide to hunt back towards the trailer. Ron and Eddie walk across the field of stubble, heading to Uncle Bill's woods. I take the other side of the ditch. Midway through the woods Ron yells "Rooster!" and fires twice. I look up and see the bird skimming near the treetops. If he turns my way, I have him. But he doesn't.

Later, sitting in the trailer over a beer and a bowl of chili, we decide things are far from ordinary. After awhile the stories start; the best part of hunting.

* * *

Later that afternoon, at Schoonover's farm, with the sun beginning to set, we crouch and wait as a flock of wood ducks circle above the drainage ditch.

"We'll let them settle in," Ron whispers to us, "and then move up and jump them."

One by one the ducks glide into the water. When the final one finishes its descent we start walking slowly— as quietly as possible— across the remaining stretch of field. That's no easy feat. The muck farm, as we called it, had been used for many years to raise potatoes. The Schoonover family, deciding to toss in the towel on farming and work fulltime hauling produce, had enrolled the land in the conservation program. The rich soil offered optimum growing conditions; the various weeds quickly turned from grasslands, then evolved into tangled undergrowth and soon islands of brush and small saplings appeared. If you had hunting dogs and stamina, this was a prime spot for bird hunting.

When we reach our destination, a few ducks, sensing our presence, take off. Eddie fires first and downs a bird. The rest of them fly wildly off the water. Ron fires and bags another one while I miss my shot. Then another part of the flock rises up and goes behind us. I turn, fire my shotgun, and hit one. We fan out and pick up the downed birds. They are beautiful looking with their brightly-colored feathers.

"That's the thing about wood ducks," Ron says to me. "Once they make up their minds to land, that's it. Any other kind of duck would have probably spooked."

With the evening descending, I head for home to clean my bird.

* * *

The following week the weather has warmed. Early in the afternoon I drive over to Grant Road and park. After loading the gun, I take off across the hayfield towards the marsh. Most people have a special place: The camper, a special site; the fisherman, a special lake or stream; or the canoeist, a special river. This marsh is mine. No hunting season would be complete without a walk through it.

The first one occurred when I was 13. My father and I had just started the evening milking. “Why don’t you take the gun and go out and see if you can get a pheasant,” Dad said to me matter-of-factly. I looked at him, partly stunned and partly disbelieving. I’d badgered him about letting me hunt with a gun since I was 11 and, in turn, had been repeatedly told to “wait until you’re older.” Now, out of the clear blue, with no warning, the longed-for moment had arrived.

So I took off, shotgun in hand, with our dog Duke trailing behind. I started through the corn field in back of the barns towards this marsh. On the way, I even had a bird fly up ahead of me and fired the gun. While the bird was in no danger of getting hit and the noise sent Duke scampering home, I gotten my first taste of *the hunt*. Each autumn, when I return, the place still seems to be the same. The tall oak, the poplars, the fallen logs, and the heavy line of brush are seemingly timeless. My sentiment for this place is, I suppose, the aspect of hunting that’s less a sport and perhaps more of a ritual. It’s my personal rite to the outdoors; my homage to nature.

Recalling the '68 Campaign

There was another election, eight years ago in 1968. More climactic, it was to become a watershed of sorts. A finale for the events that preceded it.

During the summer and early fall of that year, my sister, two high school friends, and I had campaigned for Wes Vivian, the Democratic candidate for the 2nd Congressional District. On election night we drove to Ann Arbor and spent the evening at the UAW Hall, watching the returns come in. The Democrats there had little anticipation of winning the seat. Vivian was losing (as expected) to the incumbent Marvin Esch, while Vice President Hubert Humphrey was being narrowly defeated by Richard Nixon. The closeness of the presidential vote was due, in part, to the candidacy of former Alabama governor, George Wallace who ran under the American Independent Party banner and presumably took votes from Nixon.

Vivian appeared at the hall early in the evening where he talked briefly with friends, and soon left. He re-appeared, exchanged "hellos" with us, but again stayed only a short time. Eventually, with no victory party to attend, the four of us drove back to Fowlerville. Vivian had been elected four years before, during Lyndon Johnson's landslide win over Barry Goldwater. In that election, he edged out the longtime incumbent, George Meader, with a tally of just over 50 percent of the vote. Two years later Vivian lost the seat to Esch in another close race. In '68 he charted a comeback after Robert Kennedy's presidential announcement, casting his fortunes with those of Kennedy.

The Senator's death took the heart from his campaign and left him in a sort of political limbo. Given his name recognition, he defeated two other candidates in the primary. One of them, John McDermott, had aligned himself with Humphrey, while the other, Jerome Dupont, jumped into the race as a supporter of U.S. Senator Gene McCarthy. When the Chicago Convention split the Democrats, Vivian (like Humphrey) did not have a fully unified campaign apparatus behind him going into the fall. The district, which included my home area of Livingston County, leaned Republican, so there was that obstacle. Then, given the turmoil of the past couple of years, along with the roller-coaster sequence of events that occurred during 1968, independents and even many Democrats were in no mood for the message championed by Vivian and the late senator.

There has always been the "what if" aspect about Robert Kennedy's presidential bid. What if he hadn't been killed? What if he had gone on to win the nomination? What if his message of closing the gaps between young and old, rich and poor, and black and white; of ending the war; of providing governmental help to the poor and disadvantaged; and of giving legal protection to those suffering from discrimination... what if this message of compassion and reconciliation had resonated enough to win a race against Nixon? But even before Kennedy's death and certainly afterwards, a backlash was forming. Many voters were reacting in fear and anger to the chaos and to what they judged as a threat to traditional values, social stability, and respect for law and order. Given that perceived reality and with Kennedy dead, in a newsman's words, Vivian headed toward the election "as if approaching the last act of a Greek tragedy."

A lot had occurred since the '66 election, ranging from the tragic upheavals in several American cities (including the '67 riot in Detroit that left 43 dead) to what the media called a youth rebellion that manifested itself with such symbols as long hair, hard rock music, sexual promiscuity, and marijuana use.

Foremost, though, of what had happened, was the widening of the American war effort. American soldiers had increasingly taken over the burdens of combat, with the number of casualties mounting as a consequence, while the B-52s went from supply lines along the Ho Chi Minh Trail into the heartland of North Vietnam. This build-up brought strong opposition, with college students being in the forefront with their anti-war teach-ins and rallies. The country began to split between those who supported the direction of the war and its stated purpose and those who opposed its continuation.

This opposition was echoed and found voice in the halls of Congress. In November of 1967, Minnesota Senator Eugene McCarthy revealed his decision to challenge President Johnson. He told newsmen at the time that he hadn't "any illusions of taking the nomination from the president, rather the purpose is to reverse in the current Vietnam policy."

In late January came the shock of the Tet Offensive, with the Viet Cong capturing parts of several South Vietnamese cities and, in doing so, undermining many of the political and military statements that Johnson had put forth. A month later McCarthy pulled a near upset against Johnson in the New Hampshire Primary, exposing the President's political vulnerability. A day afterwards Senator Robert Kennedy entered the race.

Two weeks later, the situation drastically changed when Johnson announced his decision to both de-escalate the war and to step down from the presidency. Martin Luther King was murdered four days later, and many cities were wracked with violent disorders. Then, within two months, in early June, only moments after addressing his jubilant supporters about his win in the California Primary, Kennedy was also assassinated.

The remainder of the year was highlighted by, amongst other things, the near toppling of the French government by students and workers, the beginnings of armed conflict in Northern Ireland, the Russian invasion of Czechoslovakia, the violence at the Democratic Convention between demonstrators and the Chicago police, the marriage of Jackie Kennedy to Aristotle Onassis, and finally the Christmas Eve flight around the moon of three astronauts on Apollo 8.

* * *

Now, eight years later, the events of '68 (and the period before it) seem like faded photographs. Other elections have been held; other candidates have emerged. A new president, Jimmy Carter of Georgia, is poised to take over from President Gerald Ford, the man he just recently defeated in a close vote. Marvin Esch has joined the ranks of defeated politicians in an unsuccessful bid for the U.S. Senate against Don Reigle. McCarthy, who once toppled a president in the snows of New Hampshire, barely mustered one percent of the national vote in his independent bid for that office this time around. Nixon had already left the center stage, his presidency disgraced in the aftermath of Watergate, while Humphrey, standing in the wings this spring in hopes of another chance at high office, waited too long.

The issues of eight years ago are now largely history, replaced by different concerns, priorities and issues. No doubt, in another eight years, when the year 1984 rolls around, the same will hold true for many of our present-day difficulties, worries, and challenges.

Certainly, elections provide drama with the spectacle of two people struggling for power; and, after the vote is counted, the rise of one at the expense of the other. We are a nation that relishes our assorted competitions. Maybe the greater drama is found in the individual voter; the feelings and thoughts that each person brings with them as he or she enters the polling booth, coupled with the enormity of millions doing the same. The philosopher Alfred North Whitehead once suggested that "It is the business of the future to be dangerous." Maybe so, but it is not an attitude that many embrace. Facing that future is each person's private tug-of-war. We do so with boldness, or reluctance, and with a vision of what we wish to see happen or a reaction against what we fear might occur. But in fairness, maybe we bring a little of both to our decisions and preferences.

Elections, candidates, compelling issues, and all of the rest of the panorama of self-governance, bold and vivid at this moment, will indeed fade into the past, replaced by a different cast of characters and a fresh story line. Even so, what we discuss, and what we ultimately decide with the current campaign, matters greatly. It mattered in 1968 and it mattered in 1976. Who prevails and how each of us faces tomorrow's uncertainties have consequences. The cumulative outcome will, in some manner or another, influence our options and direction as we move onward, individually and as a larger society.

This River Never Forgets

We return again. Like sailors come back to a favorite port. To the worn path that trails through the stand of brush to the river. You walk along it, a pole in hand, some refreshments stuffed in the vest pockets, feeling again that stir of anticipation. Others are already fishing. They sit on upturned buckets or rest on the grassy bank, their lines bowing slightly in the current despite weighted-down leaders.

The sunlight here reflects dully off the clay-colored waters that drift by. It simmers as well above the trees that line the opposite bank and over the farm land beyond. There is the familiar smell, a mingle of river mud, rotting logs and greenery. A familiar stillness also, broken only by an occasional voice or passing car.

Downriver, they have a song about the Red Cedar. About tree-shaded banks, the smell of lilac, warm October nights, and the remembrance of a long-ago love. But here along the stretch above the Gamby Bridge, and further on along the creeks and streams that feed the main river, one sees instead the last traces of still untamed country. The dark recesses of surrounding forest, the flooded marshlands, the tangle of torn vines and swale.

The years have brought changes to this river. There are, of course, the ones that accompany each season. The swift current of the spring thaw, the slow lingering of the summer months, the cold darkness that comes with the first snows. And there are the subtle ones of nature. The slow etchings of passing time, witnessed in a fallen tree or the gradual undercutting of a bank.

More importantly, though, are the changes that have occurred within us; they provide an evolving perspective when we come back each year.

There is the distant memory of trailing behind my father as he went down the lane in back of the farm to spear frogs. We would walk alongside the shallow creek that forked into the river; he moving cautiously through the marsh grass and cattails at the edge while I remained up on the high bank. The river and the thick forest on its far side had an eerie, forbidding look. Later, when I was a little older and came here alone, I always stayed on the sandy meadow where the foxes dug their burrows or else in the nearby woods that the pasturing cattle kept cleared of undergrowth.

There was the winter many years later when I had little work and even less money. Walking through those same trees, hearing only the snow crunching underfoot, and the wind rattling the remaining oak leaves on the branches, I could momentarily forget my unpleasant circumstances. Instead, I had the snowy landscape to consider, and the rabbit tracks to study for freshness.

There was a Christmas morning a couple of years later when I decided to go hunting prior to the family gathering. The wind blew sharply over the barren hayfield, numbing the fingertips. Once inside the covering of the forest, the sound became muffled. I walked for awhile and then stopped for a smoke. Beyond, past the bare trees, were the fields and fence rows. Further on stood the outbuildings and the farm house where so much of my youth had been spent.

In the spring, during those years when I lived there, the chill air greeted me as I cut across the pasture to herd the cows for their morning milking. The grass would be wet from the heavy dew and, with the first light of dawn, a thick fog would form over the drainage ditch to the south and hover above the bordering marshland.

I grew up hearing the stories of the wild dog packs that raided the neighboring livestock, mostly sheep and chickens, and hid out in the wild places. There were also stories of the huckleberry swamps that existed, yet I could never seem to find them. I would listen at the dinner table to tales of the people who had lived here in earlier times, many of them family members; all of them gone now, resting in small out-of-the-way graveyards.

So many of my hopes and aspirations were born and nurtured on this farm and nearby countryside. Most were the imaginings of boyhood, full of glitter and sparkle. I daydreamed of grand adventures, great accomplishments, and exotic locales that would come my way when I became older and was on my own. Until then, I kept them guarded inside like a buried treasure. One day, I told myself, my dreams would come true. Yet, adulthood arrived, the years went by, and most of the aspirations slipped away. Unrealistic. Pie-in-the sky. Fanciful. Was it youth, or just ignorance, or perhaps some hidden conceit that gave to me a belief I could mold the awaiting future to fit my vision? The hard knocks of the real world, the unexpected twists and turns of daily living, the slow etchings of passing time, have (each and all) altered the mental landscape, left the vision somewhat tattered and a little worse for the wear; there to be remembered fondly for the promises it once held, but never became.

Like the physical environment around us, we change. We adapt. In the place of those youthful daydreams, new hopes and aspirations — more modest in ambition—emerged. A few of them have even come true.

If you return to the river at night there is no fishing, only the dark outline of the trees around you. The water's surface is an intermixture of reflected moonlight and shadows. A steady hum of crickets and insects permeates the otherwise still surroundings. A thousand stars flicker in the sky above.

In the cloak of darkness and the reverie of thought, the pattern of those bygone years spread out. You think of what might have been, and wonder why you went this way and not that way? For a moment, the magical sense of possibility returns; all of those wonderful hopes that accompanied a boy as he did the farm chores, drove the tractor, read the books, tossed the ball against the barn, and watched the movies and TV shows. They hover once more in the mind's eye, seemingly within grasp, their possibility as real now as they once were. Yet not real. Only *what might have beens*. Gone like wisps of smoke in a spring wind.

You seek a pause, another moment or two to gaze a little longer upon them. But this river never forgets, nor should we, that the worn path that leads through the stand of brush to its grassy bank does not take us back to a familiar yesterday, only ahead to an uncertain tomorrow.

Life in the Detroit Lions Press Box

September 1977. Ah, yes. The Detroit Lions press box in the Pontiac Silverdome. I always knew that I belonged here in the big time, covering pro football.

The fact that I'm supposed to be covering the Howell High School Marching Band's halftime performance (which is the reason I got a pass to sit in the press box) is beside the point. None of the other newsmen are aware of that. For all they know, I might be covering this game for the Associated Press or *Sports Illustrated.*

Former star quarterback Earl Morrall doesn't know that. He just came up and asked if he could borrow the extra chair at my table.

"Sure," I tell him.

Former Lion linebacker Mike Lucci doesn't know it either. He just walked by looking mean and Italian. (I make a mental note to start doing some sit-ups). Nor is former *Free Press* sports editor Lyall Smith, who just gave me a roster of the teams, privy to my real assignment.

Enough of this name-dropping though.

The reason I'm sitting at the table is because I'm partaking of the free food and beer that the Lions provide at the lounge, located behind the press box. When you cover high school football, namely Fowlerville High School football, you have to pay for your hot dogs and pop. Not in the Lions press box; it's all the beef stroganoff and Pabst your stomach can hold.

The Lions even provide waitresses, so none of us newsmen will get too tired walking up to the counter for more free refreshments. After all, we have to watch the game. It's part of our job. Not that we really do have to watch the game. I soon learn that at the end of each quarter the Lions provide us with a mimeographed sheet, giving the complete play-by-play sequence. Then, at the end of the half, they offer a complete statistical breakdown.

Conceivably, a reporter could spend the whole game getting bombed in the lounge and still write an accurate account of the game. Not that anyone does, though. You see, the Lions let us take our refreshments into the press box. Plus, the press box is equipped with cushioned chairs. Also, the waitresses come around during the action, asking if any of us would like a refill. So, why sit in the lounge when we have all the comforts in the box.

At halftime, in case the beef stroganoff we had during pregame wasn't enough, the Lions offer a choice of egg salad, roast beef, and tuna fish sandwiches. Nothing but the best for us sports pontiffs! Yup, with this kind of treatment, you won't catch me knocking the Lions. If Joe Falls and Al Ackerman want to, that's their business. Me? I'd just as soon be invited back. I'm not going to say anything about Detroit's sloppy defense against the Cleveland rush or make jokes about the punter.

Instead, I grab a tuna fish and announce that the Lions' offense is certainly looking sharp. I'm a quick learner, you see. I've spent too much time at prep school games with frozen toes and numb fingers not to understand the comforts of a climate-controlled stadium. Also, I've pushed and shoved through too many pimple-faced kids crowded in front of the concession stand, trying to buy a Coke before the halftime intermission is over, not to appreciate the difference when a lovely lady asks me if I'd like another drink.

Covering high school ball is hard ground compared with this feathered pro bed. And it so happens that I like feathered beds, along with easy work, free food, play-by-play sequence sheets, complete stats, free beer, pretty waitresses, and rubbing elbows with sports stars.

This is one dog that won't bite the hand that feeds him. If the Lions want me to cover their games, I'm here, hat-in-hand, ready to please; a 'yes' man who'd be smart enough not to tell William Clay Ford how to run his Pussycats.

The DJ Returns

"Night Flight 760. I'm Jay Roberts, your host and captain. Tonight's destination is…"

Countless nights I've fallen asleep to the mellow voice of WJR's late-evening disc jockey, and his even more mellow musical selections. On several unfortunate mornings, I've even awakened to the sound of Roberts' voice. Not surprisingly, he always sounds better at 11:30 p.m. than he does at 5:30 a.m.

The radio disc jockey is both a familiar and obscure figure. His or her voice, over the years, becomes a soothing, comforting friend; a constant companion while you're traveling, at work, or just bored. I remember driving up from New Orleans late one night a few years back. I'd been listening to a succession of DJs during the long route when I finally got WJR in southern Indiana. Hearing Jay's voice, despite being a couple of hundred miles away from Michigan, was the same as making it home.

Still, despite that familiarity, the radio man is a stranger. All you know of him, even after many years, is the sound of his vocal pipes. I remember the first time I saw pictures of J.P. McCarthy and sportscaster Bob Reynolds. I had this odd sensation of their faces not belonging to those well-known, resonant voices.

I started listening to pop-music radio stations at the age of ten. This was in the early '60s, the eve of The Beatles mania. My initial impetus was caused by James Darren and his hit single "Goodbye Cruel World." I had seen him on the Donna Reed Show, playing Mary Stone's romantic interest. The plot line had him portraying a pop star who had to say "good bye" to Mary because he would soon be joining the Army. When he sang the song, the word "service" was put in place of "circus."

After that, every possible chance I got, I'd rotate the AM dial in search of Darren's lamenting tune. No doubt, by doing so, it was inevitable that I would soon fall under the spell of the disc jockeys and their "Top 40s" jargon and play lists. The DJ was the musical guru in those *American Graffiti* years. While nationally Bobby Rydell, Ricky Nelson, and Connie Francis may have reigned, locally, the radio record spinner was the celebrity.

WXYZ's Dave Prince was popular enough to have his own Saturday afternoon TV show on Channel 7, while Eric-O and Gene Healy of WILS in Lansing were surefire drawing cards at any mid-Michigan high school dance.

The ultimate objective was to peddle the 45s. I still remember the envy I felt whenever I came into contact with someone who had accumulated a vast record pile. As we know, the arrival of The Beatles to the shores of New York in 1964 changed the then existing pop music scene. As the sun rose for the lads from Liverpool, along with such groups as The Rolling Stones, The Yardbirds, and The Animals, the limelight simultaneously faded for the AM disc jockeys as well as the era of Fabian, Frankie Avalon, and Sandra Dee.

Home-grown musicians, inspired by The Beatles' example, began forming their own rock groups. Dance committees were soon depleting their treasuries for such drawing cards as The Rationals, The Bob Seger System, and Mitch Ryder and the Detroit Wheels rather than Dave Prince and the boys.

In addition, the 45s began giving way, more and more, to the long-playing album for teenaged fans, while the upstart FM radio, featuring voiceless record spinners, and only an occasional commercial, began attracting a growing number of listeners.

But what goes around comes around. The salad days of the DJ may be returning. The format of FM radio has changed during the last decade to include more of the DJ's personality. Ears are now tuned to the baritone vibes of WRIF's Arthur Penhallow, or the intimate-sounding Sally Victor of WFMK. Also, venues featuring live music are getting stiff competition from the platter-oriented disco bars. Once again, and rightly so, the DJ is the "big man" with the audience.

More importantly, Fabian recently appeared on a *Lavern and Shirley* TV episode. Nostalgia for the good, old days (pre-1964) is emerging. Can James Darren be far behind?

* * *

Jay Roberts replies to column

To Steve Horton:

Would you believe, I opened an envelope from Harold Smith of Stewardson, Ill. and out popped your article of Nov. 30, 1977? It came as quite a nice surprise and very pleasant Christmas message. Thank you very much!

I'm enclosing a pic. I think the face & voice match—so there.

Happy season,'

Jay

At the End of a Fishing Trip

It was Sunday morning, in late May, and I was at the marina on Sutton's Bay. I had been on a week-long fishing trip, having taken a vacation from my newspaper job. In the previous days, I had tried my luck at several spots in and around Traverse City. But on this, my final day, the only attempts to catch a fish were being made by several sea gulls flying aimlessly above. The waters before me had a greenish-blue tinge. A faint breeze rippled the surface. Over by the docks several men worked on their boats, while in the distance, the greenery of the Old Mission Peninsula simmered faintly in the early light.

There was a translucent quality to the setting: an observation made perhaps more from thought than actuality. This was a familiar place, a scenic vista that I had enjoyed on previous visits. I had repeated the memory of being here in my mind's eye during the preceding weeks in eager anticipation of this return. But now, finally sitting on a bench beside the shoreline, the air fresh and sea-scented, there was not the expected contentment, only a disquieting feeling of misplacement.

The sea can often be an uncanny mirror. That day, in the overcast of the morning, caught in the place's solitude, it reflected an unexpected mood of melancholy. The night before I had gone to Sleder's Tavern, visiting with my friend who lived in Traverse City. During the two years that I'd lived in the city, I'd gotten to know various people. But, after leaving, Randy was the only one I kept in touch with. We had both been cooks at the Big Boy restaurant, working the night shift. He and I along with others on the crew had socialized after work, and through that association of work and play the two of us had become good friends.

Over drinks we had done the usual kidding, our talk touching mostly on our shared past— a rehash of mutual acquaintances and experiences. In retrospect, we had resembled a pair of aging comrade-in-arms, reminiscing about our glorious youth with little else in common. Separated by the distance of geography and more gradually by the passing weeks, our paths had begun to diverge. We no longer shared today, only yesterday.

He had moved to the area shortly before I had, stayed on, and married. Now his wife and he were expecting their first baby in the autumn. I, on the other hand, with a chance to help start a newspaper, had left; chose instead to return home, going back to other, better-known faces.

There are some lessons that come hard. Yet by learning and accepting them, perhaps they can strengthen us, or at least offer better explanations of personal motivation. Since leaving Traverse City, I had nurtured the idea that I would soon be back. However, each successive visit to the place had found fewer and fewer ties that still bound until now there was only a friend and pleasant recollections.

Even so, living in the city had proved an important interlude. I had moved here in the spring of 1974, searching for another new beginning. Yearning, I suppose, for some revelation on how I could, or should, live my life. None came— but it was here that I had begun living on my own initiative. It was here that I had survived grief, gone back to writing, enjoyed the company of new acquaintances, and felt the sublime beauty and majestic sweep of the land.

Traverse City had been a place to pause, take stock, and then grow. Despite that, I had abandoned it without hesitation, succumbing to personal and ancestral echoes, a benign siren's call, if you will, in what's now become a familiar pattern of roaming and returning home that has marked the ten years since completing high school.

Truths, I believe, rarely come as sudden revelations. More often they flicker on the outskirts of vision, there to be discerned gradually, or to fade away unnoticed. And so, at the end of a fishing trip, a thought occurred to me, and the truth moved into clearer view. If we can say there are people who need the roots and permanence of home and others who are afflicted by a compulsion to roam, then there must also be those who are caught between the two passions: victims of an inexplicable tug-of-war between restlessness and the ties of the past.

Each of us makes our choices— either for fortune or misfortune — that bind us to a course and ultimately create the pattern we live by. If we can build our own heavens and hells, then perhaps we can also opt for a purgatory that gives us a taste of each of those extremes, but as yet with no commitment. Which passion prevails, which sentiment tugs the hardest, I guess will be determined by the passing years, and all of the future choices that are made in combination with past ones.

So on this Sunday morning I saw my particular course, and remembered those various decisions that had led me to this quiet beach and to this moment… each and all a part of my emerging pattern.

And I recalled a line that I had penned several years before while living in San Francisco; one of my first attempts to escape, only to return.

It went: "Orange streaks over the foggy eastern shore, pierces through this soft parade of summer smoke… in the distance the light of home."

Perhaps I had known all along.

A Country Christmas

On Christmas Eve we would hurry about with the milking, needing to finish up so we could get to church for the early service. The string of musical carols played on the radio; the songs were intermingled with the mooing Holsteins and accompanied by the steady beat of the milk pump.

Above our milking area was the hay mound, along with the bales of straw. I would go up and push the loose hay down the chute that was located near the stairway and then shove several bales of straw down the other chute that was located above the holding pen where the cows rested at night. Afterwards I fed them hay and spread the straw around the pen for bedding.

A farm always seemed an appropriate place to spend this particular night. Like most kids, I'd have preferred occupying the early evening up at the house watching TV, but the excitement of the occasion overwhelmed the usual reluctance I felt about chores.

There remains a faint outline of memory from when I was very young – probably four or five – and attending a candlelight service. We sat in the back of the church, and I felt the wonder of holding a lighted candle, and seeing the dark room aglow with flickering flames. No doubt the congregation was singing *Silent Night*.

The early Christmas Eve service usually involved several of the children performing as a chorus or re-enacting the Nativity Story. That's the one we went to, including the year I took part. I believe I had a non-speaking role as a shepherd. Earlier that day, or the day before, we'd stop to see my great-grandparents, Rollin and Blanche. They lived a couple of miles away, around the corner, in an old farmhouse. The only holiday tree they had, within my limited recall, was a small artificial one, colored pink, which sat on a table, Mammy, as the family called her (rather than Blanche) had her array of modest gifts spread out on the bed in the spare room, presents for the sizable brood of children, grandchildren, and great-grandchildren. As each of us showed up— sometime during those days before or on Christmas Day— she'd go in and get our gift. Grandpa Rollin kept his normal vigil, sitting in his rocker in front of the wood stove at the end of the kitchen, content to visit with the steady stream of relatives and leave the business of gifts to his mate.

At home, on Christmas morning, the wait always seemed to last forever. The fantasy world of a decorated tree, surrounded by colorfully wrapped presents, tested a youngster's patience. There was the contrary pull of wanting the magic to last, but also wanting to discover what the presents contained. My sister, Carol, and younger brother, Craig, shared the long wait. My father co-operated by cutting short his regular morning chores, normally done after the milking and before breakfast— postponing them until later. He'd come up to the house, change his clothes, and then proceed with the task of passing out our gifts. My mother kept busy taking pictures of us.

After the gifts were torn open, we ate breakfast. Then there were those delayed morning chores to complete. Later, back in the house, I had time to examine my holiday bounty. Everyone took turns in the bathtub, got dressed, and we headed over to Grandpa and Grandma Horton's place. They also lived just around the corner from us, only in the opposite direction from Mammy and Grandpa Rollin. Arriving, we joined aunts, uncles, our cousins, and Great Grandpa Bement.

My granddad regaled us with stories and jokes as Grandma scurried about, putting food on the table and checking the status of potatoes, gravy, salads, rolls, the dressing bowls, and the turkey platters. My mother and aunts (who had helped prior to the meal) would insist she sit down and enjoy her effort. Eventually she did—about midway through the feast; but even then she continuously surveyed the table to make sure nothing was amiss.

For a few years "we" older cousins, for space reasons, had our own table in the kitchen or the wash room, away from the main family. The arrangement gave us opportunity to do plenty of laughing and goofing around; a reaction that, in turn, kept our respective mothers nervous, and periodically coming in to check on the situation.

After the meal there came the seemingly endless period of waiting for the dishes to be washed and packed away. Only when this chore was finished could the presents then be opened. The tree always stood in the corner of the living room next to the front door; that entrance hardly ever being used by family or visitors. Adding to the holiday setting were the burning logs in the fireplace, the wood crackling from the heat. The area near it would be quite hot.

With the highlight of opening the presents finally completed, "we" kids played with our various gifts. In the late afternoon, it was milking time again. Then, when that was finished, we all had supper from various leftovers, visited and played some more, and finally the day ended.

* * *

The once vivid images those long-ago Christmases have now blurred into a pleasant, slow-spinning kaleidoscope of recollection. They help generate an internal light which reignites as each Christmas season returns. I have little doubt that the spark that first ignited this personal light, our particular and special feeling about December 25th, originates from those tender years. How we experience Christmas as a young child— what we're taught, what we see and sense— will determine our feelings about it in later adulthood.

This internal light is perhaps the balance needed to offset the seeming chaos of all the external yuletide trappings. Without this counter influence, or with too little of it, the season can turn into mere clutter and noise. But this inner light, when illuminated by all of the other symbols and messages of *true meaning* available to us, combine to give Christmas a radiant glow.

The customs, traditions, and habits of our family are special to us, but probably pretty similar to what others did. We were farmers and lived in the country. For me, this upbringing and background will always be the prevailing image of Christmas.

When I was young and still only saw the trees and not the forest, those annual seasons of celebration seemed to stretch out in an endless line of past and future. The inevitable differences that come from growing older never seemed to affect the core. But time did alter it; ever so gradually at first and then, seemingly in the blink of an eye, forever. Family members died, and the rest of us moved up a rung on the generational ladder. A way of life and pattern of routine that seemed enduring was, alas, fleeting and fragile. Now, as adults, the Christmas celebration centers on our children. Hopefully, the light being sparked within them will be as precious as the one first ignited within us.

Of all the gifts under the Christmas tree, none match the gift of memory… the remembrances of those times we shared together. We'll share some more again this Christmas— and add to our bounty.

A Trip on the Platte River

It happened from a set of haphazard circumstances which, I suppose, is more often the case than not. 'Cousin' Clem Spillane and I had driven to Hell on Saturday forenoon for their 'Almost Anything Goes' festivities and ended up that evening in Traverse City on a fishing trip. The fishing part, though, turned out to be incidental. Instead, we wound up spending our Sunday afternoon on a leisurely canoe trip down the Platte River to Lake Michigan.

I'd like to say that this occurrence typifies my lifestyle, but it doesn't. I canoed once before, when I was 19, and found it uneventful, producing only sore shoulder muscles. I've passed by dozens of canoe liveries since then and never pictured myself floating casually along the current, scanning the wooded banks. Fortunately, 'Cousin' Clem is persuasive, so we rented a canoe at Riverside, a livery northwest of Honor, packed a few refreshments, and headed downstream.

The trip lasted about two hours and covered a winding course of approximately seven miles. No doubt there are more picturesque and secluded places to canoe in the state, but for a beginner it was fun and, more importantly, relaxing. Much of the river runs through a low marshy area. Birch, scrub pine, and some cedar blanket the shores. Fallen logs litter the edges. Later, at the journey's end, is the magnificent sweep of the Lake Michigan shoreline… the sand bluffs to the north, the pale-blue waters fanning outward, and the sun-soaked reefs.

There were moments of absolute stillness during the trek; also pleasantries exchanged with other canoeists, and even some aggravation.

The aggravation came in the form of a motor boat, equipped with a stereo tape deck. The operator had started off with our convoy, but decided to go back and forth as he journeyed down the river, and had passed us a couple of times. The presence of the motor boat, besides proving annoying, also points to a major difficulty looming for recreation in Michigan… the sharing of limited resources and areas by an increasing number of different and sometimes incompatible users.

I thought as we floated along the current how nice it would be to fish certain stretches we were passing and realized that it would be hard to do so with the canoes going by. Obviously, courtesy and empathy go a long way toward the harmonious sharing of a river or recreational area. It's perhaps also important to remember that someone else's enjoyment and pleasure may, through haphazard circumstances, become your own.

Golden Slumbers & the 60's

(Note: This piece was written in 1980, shortly after 'Beatle' John Lennon's murder)

They took the country by storm in 1964, appearing on *The Ed Sullivan Show*, and what followed was a cultural and generational outburst that proved unique, probably never to be repeated. They ended that career as a musical group in 1969 with the album *Abbey Road,* and with *Golden Slumbers*, a song about a longing for home.

Eleven years later one of them, John Lennon, was murdered in a barrage of gunfire outside his New York City apartment house.

Much has been written about Lennon and The Beatles in the days since that incident. They were a phenomenon, riding the crest of a giant rebellious wave that swept the country, altering many lives. Their deepest influence obviously was felt by those of us who grew up during that time span. Their music and lifestyle helped to explain and even articulate the changes our age group was experiencing, and smooth out many of the rough edges.

But, while conceding their great impact on music and teenaged culture, there was much more to the '60s than The Beatles. Most chroniclers seem to mark President Kennedy's assassination as the watershed that began the decade. If you need an end, my own would be the overwhelming defeat of George McGovern's liberal Democratic candidacy in 1972. In between most of the country, and the youth in particular, found themselves on a wild ride that, when it ended, left many exhausted and somewhat dazed.

The Vietnam War (and the ensuing movement to stop it) overshadowed most of the decade. But landmark events included the civil rights movement, the War on Poverty, urban riots, college campus demonstrations, the assassinations of Martin Luther King and Robert Kennedy, the political forces of George Wallace and Richard Nixon, the emergence of the hippie lifestyle, the backlash of the Silent Majority, the trauma of the Chicago Convention in 1968, the student deaths at Kent State, the use of drugs, the environmental movement, and the various musical trends that emerged after The Beatles' debut.

It was a decade of constant change, of forces working with and against each other. It began on a note of tragedy, peaked, ebbed, and then, I believe, sank from its own turbulence. In the midst of the commotion and upheaval, serving as a symbol of the youthful angst, were The Beatles. With songs, the length of their hair, and their evolving beliefs, the lads from Liverpool, proved to be both leaders and followers. Their example created trends, but, like the rest of us, the unfolding chronology of episodes altered their course. They both acted and re-acted to the unfolding events.

There were various avenues of self discovery as well as discontent taken in the '60s'. Some began with hope and ended in disillusionment, or tragedy. Some found only a dead end. Many tired of the effort and chose a different, less demanding path. Others are still walking straight ahead, facing the obstacles, steadfast to the ideals that first inspired them to seek a newer, better world.

We know Lennon's road because it was public and because so many of us started out by going in a similar direction. The turns and twists his journey took were the same ones many others experienced. I find it interesting that in Lennon's final record album, *Double Fantasy*, he extolled the traditional values of marriage and raising a son. From rebellious youth and the need for change to middle age and the contentment of family, perhaps John Lennon did find a way to get back home.

The Hunter Does Not Always Hunt

A false assumption many make is that a hunter always hunts for game; or, when he does hunt, he seeks only that.

Rabbits— those creatures of Easter lore and Warner Brothers cartoons— have speed, agility, and stealth which, more times than not, leave them safe from us average-to-mediocre shots. Still, rabbit hunting is a great sport, even if you sometimes have to stop off at the grocery store for the stew's main ingredient. It's healthy exercise — a consideration which always gives one a mental boost. Plus, there's something cleansing and refreshing that comes over you as you move slowly through snowbound woods, eyes peeled for recent tracks, or the movement of a cottontail.

During those late mornings and early afternoons the air is cold and biting, but the walk keeps you warm. Behind me, stretching across the snowy tract is the path of foot marks, testimony that— like the journey of a thousand miles— we begin and end with single steps. The woods in back of the farm is always a good place to hunt, with plenty of brush piles and undergrowth and a thick outer edge of trees which keeps the snows from drifting in. There are different ways to hunt the area; various routes you can take, circling over there, or cutting across here. On the high ground is the stand of maple, recently logged, the tree tops still scattered about. Further on is the low clearing of marsh grass, with clusters of poplar saplings, then the drainage ditch which flows into the Red Cedar River. Flanking the ditch to the northwest are more woods. Occasionally, you'll see a rabbit hopping slowly ahead, its ears alert for possible dangers. Sometimes, walking though the underbrush, a partridge will flush, bursting suddenly out of the snowy nest.

If stray dogs have run the woods, then the hunting is ruined. The smooth surface of white has been churned up, and the rabbits are well-hidden in their lairs. Otherwise, the snow covering is marred only by the imprints of passing or frolicking wildlife. Whatever route that's taken, the midpoint of the hunt is where the ditch forks into the river. There you can sit and smoke some tobacco, rest against a tree, the coat spread beneath to keep you dry, and the shotgun propped up against the nearby tree. Just upstream lays the large oak that has fallen into the river, the rippling waters eddy around its branches and during the colder weather, ice floes form.

There is always a pervasive quietness to this spot, a stillness that permeates you. For a few minutes the urge to get up and leave is strong, a momentum caused by busy days and hurried activities that fill and clutter the mind. We move even when not moving. You work hard, and usually play too hard. Life becomes a noisy affair or else the impatient wait for the noise. At this place though, watching the river, the forest silent in its colorless shroud, the quieter rhythms come forth… those soft chords that now, finally listened to, can be heard.

Here is the slow, steady tension of constant renewal— a place of beginnings and ends, and of beginnings again. Here, fish feed and rivers flow, pine cones fall and foxes move along the field's edge. Here, thistles bloom and whither, breezes stir, and past and present blend together into a moment. Here, too, if you are fortunate and wait long enough, battered hopes become refreshed again.

The ground stretches white into the forest's dark recesses. Overhead, the branches are etched black against the winter sky. The silence remains as you rise to leave. The hunter does not always hunt just for game— and, even when he does hunt with that purpose, he sometime seeks more. Sometimes the search, like a stealthy rabbit being pursued, is for one's self.

Kennedy and Us

Every 10 years, a lot of newsprint and film footage is devoted to late November 1963. The cause, of course, is the Kennedy assassination: those four nightmarish days of tragedy and haunting emotion that were seared into our collective memory. Along with remembering this traumatic episode from our shared history, there's usually a retrospective of the man and his presidency— the various events that highlighted his administration, providing the context of the times he was both part of and influenced… the "Kennedy Years" if you will.

As individuals and families, most of us have suffered, or will eventually suffer, the death of a loved one. The accompanying pain and sorrow are similar, whether the loss is of one 90 years or only 90 days old. When a death results from the natural causes of old age, or a lingering disease, we still mourn and question, but at least we have that explanation and preparation. This scenario gives us, perhaps, a better chance at finding solace.

The unexpected death, the kind we refer to as tragic— especially of someone who's young or in the prime of life— can be harder to accept. We feel the pain of loss, but there are the added dimensions of wondering "Why?" or "How could this happen?"— the sense of death coming too soon, and of lost opportunity. When facing such grief, I suppose many of us are susceptible to justifying and rationalizing our loss by attaching an aura. We evoke metaphor; perhaps, telling ourselves that our loved one climbed higher than most, that his flame glowed more intensely, or she lived life at a more passionate pace. In doing so, what was denied in length of time was compensated by an enhanced quality. He becomes a Prince Charming or she a Fair-Haired Lady within our thoughts. We romanticize them as having been nobler, more virtuous, braver; or living life more passionately than "we" run-of-the-mill survivors.

In placing this aura over our departed loved one, we tend to deny, or at least downplay, the less glamorous reality that death came from being in the wrong place at the wrong time, from a bad mistake, poor judgment, or from weak or malfunctioning body parts. I don't know if this glossing over is good, but it's certainly human. It cushions the blow, scabs over the hurt, and allows us to go on with the necessary business of living.

I think that's what many of us who admired John Kennedy did after his assassination. He got put on a pedestal— and became the stuff of myth. The legend of Camelot became intertwined with the recounting of his life. He had come from the rough and tumble of Boston politics, yet had the refinement of a Harvard education, plus he was Catholic— a combination that supposedly was alien to the voting majority's sensibilities. But he prevailed, stooping to conquer.

He quoted Robert Frost's poetry, laced his comments with a dry and self-depreciating humor, and joked that he was the man who accompanied Jackie Kennedy to Paris. He had been a war hero, had written a best-selling book on political courage, and relaxed by sailing in the seas off of Hyannis Port. Kennedy, in addition, was young and handsome (at least compared to his predecessors, Harry Truman and Dwight Eisenhower). His speeches often displayed elegance in their phrasing and imagery. His call to higher purpose, as individuals and a nation, was embraced by many, especially the younger generation.

He launched the Peace Corps, the Alliance for Progress, championed the space program, and led the world through the Cuban Missile Crisis. He supported the admittance of black students to universities in Alabama and Mississippi, invited classical musicians to perform at the White House, and negotiated a Nuclear Test Ban Treaty. When he proclaimed "I am a Berliner," he symbolized the Free World's struggle against the Soviet Union and communism.

For awhile, after his death, we remembered all of that and much more through a soft and flattering lens. He became a mythical creature, larger than life; his end and the lost possibilities, an American tragedy.

Time eroded that pedestal, and the historical lens became more focused. In the unfolding reassessment of Kennedy and the Kennedy Years, as new information has come forth and hindsight has played its usual role, some commentators have offered (what they consider) a more realistic view, with some being quite critical in their judgment. As it turned out, there were less flattering aspects to his behavior; mainly his womanizing. The details that have emerged of his apparently voracious appetite, consummated by numerous extra-marital affairs and one-night stands, may well become his epitaph to future generations.

As for public affairs, during his administration the nation became more involved in Vietnam, an entanglement that proved controversial within a few years of his death. Whether or not he'd have sent in as many troops as Lyndon Johnson did is conjecture; the fact is that he upped the ante. As for the Civil Rights Movement, while he supported the cause and as president sent in federal troops to enforce the court-ordered admission of black students, early on he was apparently a lukewarm partisan. He feared (correctly as it turned out) that support would cost the Democratic Party many of its Southern voters. His decision to go ahead with the Bay of Pigs Invasion proved a disaster, and accounts have surfaced in recent years that his brother, Robert Kennedy, as Attorney General plotted to assassinate Fidel Castro.

But all of this, the flattering and less flattering aspects of his personal behavior, the noble pursuits and the less-principled political calculations, remind us that he was human and that he ought to be remembered accordingly— a man with weaknesses and frailties common to many men; but a man who possessed the traits and instincts of higher morality. During this brief tenure as president, he may have made a few misjudgments (at least according to current retrospect), but he also led us in a bolder and more progressive direction.

* * *

There are various kinds of winners or ways of triumphing.

There are the "so called" winners who drag others down to their level, tread hard upon these unfortunate, unsuspecting, or defenseless victims, and then crow their dominance. Counterbalancing this are the vast numbers of people who, with their ongoing contributions and steadfast daily routines, sustain and enhance the amenities of civilization. Through family, work, church, school, and service, they accomplish a quieter sort of victory. Then there are those few who possess an *esprit de corps*. They're the ones who beckon us to higher levels and nobler deeds; their daring, and love of adventure, serve as beacon lights that show us the way across uncertain seas to a new shore.

There has been and continues to be debate over whether or not Kennedy was great, good, or average in comparison to other U.S. Presidents. I don't know where he now falls or where history will eventually place him on the scale, or if it even matters. I do believe that he sought excellence within himself and encouraged it from us. He stood on behalf of peace and human rights, and those other pursuits of the human spirit he called our "New Frontier." We began with him on that "journey of a thousand miles" back on a cold, wintry January day in 1961. Although we lost him early in the journey, a great many of those who started off beside him or followed his lead, have continued on.

Perhaps, when all of the words of recollection have been written, and after all those images of our yesteryears have flickered before us, those of us who admired him will admit that he didn't climb quite as high or shine as brightly or live life as passionately as we told ourselves he did after his tragic death. But we *believed* he did and, in our believing, we tried… each in our own manner to adopt those attributes. We dared to winners and, by our doing so, he won.

On Getting Married

February 16, 1985— As you read this, I'll have already been married. But, as I write these lines, it's Saturday morning, with only a few hours to go before the ceremony.

One has mixed emotions at this time, a feeling of reservation, if you will. Not about the person I'll be marrying, but about the act itself. After 33 years of somewhat comfortable bachelorhood, changing that status quo gives one pause. If it weren't for my charming wife-to-be, I'd probably be on a fast trot towards the hills at this very moment.

Marriage is, of course, more than buckling up your courage, saying "I do," and then heading off to *happily ever after*. There are the many details involved in planning both the ceremony (even a small one like ours) and the reception. Also on the list has been the job of moving out of my apartment, and into our house. Prior to this special day, visits were made to the minister, the doctor, and the county clerk; plus I needed to buy a new suit, stop at the florist, and help decorate the hall.

The days leading up to the wedding are ones of harried activity. In addition to the time and effort required to put the various aspects of the plan into action, there are always the extra concerns of whether all the "i's" have been dotted and the "t's" crossed. And all of this is going on during the normally busy schedule of work and other day-to-day tasks.

Amid this whirlwind, one is supposed to take pause and decide *what* should be put in the wedding vows, a responsibility best accomplished in quiet reflection. The vows could have been decided six months beforehand, but that seems a bit premature. One needs the nearness of the occasion to properly acquire the emotional clarity this moment and act deserves. A dozen examples are available of what someone else did and said in their wedding ceremony. All seem fine, but coming up with the right combination that expresses her feelings and my feelings, and still has a semblance of tradition, is a slow process… a contrast in itself to everything else happening during the pre-wedding period.

Still, everything else pales before this particular task. Once the two of you decide to marry, I guess it's imperative that you also decide, in expressing your vows, *why* you wish to be married, and *what* you, together, hope to bring forth in this new and different state of life. Words are everything and nothing. They can mean precisely what you desire them to, or they can mask and disguise.

A marriage ceremony has many lofty and inspiring phrases, including “eternal love,” “cherishing you forever,” “devotion and honesty to each other,” and “I take you till death do us part.” The problem is that they’ve been heard and used so often, in casual ways, that when the time comes to appropriate them for a special occasion like marriage, the vocabulary can seem shopworn. The verbal sentiments are overly familiar, too much the common property of everyone else, and not something that comes from within; not the meaningful words that are part of you and that you wish (and need) to convey to this person who will become your physical, moral, and spiritual partner. Thus, for both of you, it becomes necessary to find words that are special, meaningful, and personal.

I haven’t come up with any earthshaking ones. Others have used them before, or similar versions that express the same sentiments.

For me, and I believe my wife-to-be, it’s important to look at our marriage as a new beginning; not in the sense that the past was bad and needs to be changed, but rather that something more profound and exciting than your previous life is about to start. I hope the vows we take also express that this is a starting off point, the first important step in a journey we will share and enjoy together.

I hope the ceremony conveys that this exchange of vows is a seed we plant in our relationship; one which, with both our efforts and caring, will grow into something we can take comfort, can be proud of, and will springboard us into fuller and richer lives. I hope the words we say to each other remind us of the gift we bring to each other on this day, *the gift of ourselves*.

I hope they further remind us that, in giving and accepting this gift, we now possess something special; a possession so important that the only safe place to keep it is within our hearts.

Horton Bay & Hemingway

One quiet Sunday afternoon we headed out of Boyne City, driving northwest along the highway. There were glimpses of picturesque Lake Charlevoix which, on this day, was choppy from the stiff wind and reflected a full blue from the overcast sky. Ahead was Horton Bay, a place unknown to me as a physical entity (this being a first visit), but well-known as the principal locale in Ernest Hemingway's *Nick Adams* stories. For many years, devoted Hemingway readers and scholars have trekked to this northern Michigan resort, as they have to other places immortalized by the author, including Key West, the bullfights of Pamplona in Spain, Sun Valley in Idaho, and, of course, Paris.

Perhaps they (we) hope to encounter the muse, or just see first hand the physical landmarks and setting of what we've read in the stories and then transformed into the realm of imagination. Every now and then a feature writer joins the crowd. The usual report compares Hemingway's literary description with the current sense of place—a *then versus now* juxtaposition— along with the memories and impressions of the young fellow by those folks who were around *back then*. Good fiction, though, transcends any particular geographical place; uses it as metaphor for the universality of all human habitats and experiences. Horton Bay still sets on the shore of Lake Charlevoix— just as it did back when Hemingway was a boy— but, more importantly, the place exists for the reader whether he or she (in actuality) is gazing out a city window, looking up at rows of books, or even staring at the interior of some ship at sea.

Along with the Hemingway lure, for us, the place had the added dimension of a shared name. That's not an overwhelming reason to drive a great distance; yet, as long as we're in the neighborhood, it's cause enough to drop in for a brief visit.

Horton Bay does not disappoint. You come on to it suddenly as the road goes around a bend. There are several stately, two-story, quite roomy homes, either well-kept over the years or restored by recent owners. They're typical lakeside dwellings, possessing large screened-in porches, upper story dormers, plenty of ornate trim, and big, shady front and back yards. Behind them is a wooded hillside.

The General Store appears little changed from its construction back in 1876. The high front porch takes about 10 steps to reach. There you can relax on the bench in front of the store window, or sit at the table-and-chair by the railing. Above the porch is an equally high false front, its top rising above the actual roofline, with three small rectangular windows and horizontal clapboard siding. The establishment serves several purposes. It's a party store for area residents, as well as for passing motorists and bicyclists, offering the usual assortment of modern merchandise common to such. It's also a morning coffee shop, with a table located in front for the locals to converse. Additionally, there's a deli in back, plus a lunch counter along one side. Menu items are listed on a blackboard in chalk lettering. Offerings include breakfast biscuits, muffins, hamburgers, various deli sandwiches, hot dogs, and other similar items.

Horton Bay General Store is both a prominent tourist attraction and a historical museum, and caters accordingly with its décor and souvenirs. Old photographs of the area's early white settlers, and others that depict the natural beauty of the woods and waters are hung on the walls, while various 19th century artifacts are displayed around the store. Intermingled with this collection is the Hemingway memorabilia, including a sketch of him as he looked at middle age with full beard. Next to the cash register are tee-shirts, with a choice between one bearing Hemingway's likeness or another featuring an etching of the store's front.

The hamlet was named after Sam Horton, a local resident and the proprietor of the store during the time when lumbering thrived in this area. Both the town and business got their start from that activity. The hills around the lake made cutting trees and sending them down towards the water an easy use of gravity. Lake Street, located a short distance from the store, was a lumber chute. Now it serves as a public access; a narrow dead-end which discourages more than a couple of parked cars. A short dock goes out into the water and on either side are privately-owned residences. Sailing craft and motor boats are anchored just off the nearby shoreline. The watercraft bob up and down in the choppy lake, turning this way-and-that from the stiff wind. In the distance is the expanse of the larger lake, surrounded by the high slopes of lush greenery.

The lumbermen, no doubt, quickly stripped the trees from these hills, leaving only stumps and piles of branches and sawdust, a fate shared by most of northern Lower Michigan in the latter years of the 1800's. But nature rebounded with the second-growth forests, and the area resumed its beauty. By Hemingway's youth in the early 1900's, the trains were bringing families to this spot, and other area lakes, for summer retreats. His father and mother, based in Oak Park outside Chicago, had a cottage on nearby Walloon Lake. It was in this vicinity that he spent his boyhood summers. He returned here to convalesce from wounds incurred on the Italian Front in World War I, and later picked this locale for his marriage ceremony with first wife Hadley.

For a few moments, I can pretend the area is not overloaded with warm-weather enthusiasts (including us) and visualize a young lad who is out and about. During his boyhood years, and as he grows older, he's soaking in the last remnants of those lumber days, learning about the neighboring Indians, experiencing the simple pursuits of hunting and fishing, having his first taste of worldly pleasures, testing himself, and pushing forward. He's understanding the joy and potential of life, but also discovering the irony of its underlying despair, and gradual slide towards death.

I can also picture him finally leaving with his young wife, and heading off to Paris. There, he would remember this place: the people encountered, the experiences shared, and the lessons offered, and turn them into prose which would live beyond his time.

So often when looking around at our surroundings, or when immersed in the repetition of daily routines, we find this familiar view and our day-to-day existence boring and uninspiring. Yet good writing, and in a broader sense good living, involves taking those seemingly mundane views and seemingly commonplace patterns of personal existence and, by altering the perception, transform them into a stimulating, interesting, and fresh perspective. It is not *what* we see and experience which motivates and inspires as much as *how* we take our look and pursue our effort. The art of good writing turns the ordinary into something extraordinary.

We leave Horton Bay— its Hemingway legacy, the place with a shared name, the lovely northern Michigan scenery— and drive back to a more familiar place, with its day-to-day routines. Perhaps upon returning, we too can alter our perspective in ways that are stimulating, interesting, and fresh.

A Child Is Born

December, 1988: The birth of an infant stands always as the centerpiece of our annual Christmas celebration. Whether that event holds a profound religious significance for you, or whether you view this holiday on more secular terms, the Christmas Story still looms large above the rest of the trappings that accompany this special season.

There is the delight of Santa and his reindeer, the various customs like decorating trees and hanging mistletoe, the enjoyment of family and friends at such events as dinners, caroling or attending concerts. We have all kinds of stories and shows that add to the richness of this tradition, be it Dr. Seuss' *Grinch* or Dickens' *Christmas Carol* or *Miracle on 34th Street*.

We recall Virginia's letter about Santa, or re-read Clement Moore's *'Twas the Night Before Christmas,* or listen to "Silent Night" whenever our Christmas Spirit needs some rekindling. In addition, we all have those many individual memories and family customs that give December its unique magic.

But always, superseding it all, all-encompassing, is the fact that "a child is born."

My wife Dawn and I had a child born on Halloween night, a baby boy, so this Christmas season, with its story of birth, is extra special. The arrival of a son, followed by the caring and tending of his basic needs, is demanding, both physically and mentally. His cycles of feeding, changing diapers, bathing, and sleeping become your routine. You soon begin to bend him a little toward your established schedule, but the changes he has brought to it are lasting and overwhelming.

While immersed in that cycle, you watch and feel your baby boy grow and mature. You wonder at his wide-eyed stare, and what sights and activities he's soaking in; you wonder, likewise, at his cries and what he's struggling against. Time is measured in days, with each day bringing more curiosity and individual personality. You realize how fleeting these moments are, and how important it is for you to enjoy what you have now rather than spend your time worrying about the future, or worse yet, thinking tomorrow holds something more magical than today.

We, to the best of our knowledge (knock very hard on wood) have a healthy, active baby. It's certainly a cliché, but, when all is said and done, that condition is very important. You hear about newborns who are physically or mentally impaired, or struck by some disease, and know how lucky you are. And, even though you know worrying about the future is usually fruitless, you can't help but hope that your baby's tomorrows are equally blessed with good health.

You also wonder a bit— when you look down at your sleeping infant— what kind of world he'll face as he grows up and, after that, what kind of opportunities and challenges he'll have as an adult. It's easy to prepare for the short-term, focusing on your hearth and home, and do your best to protect and provide. But there's uncertainty and uneasiness, especially when you consider the long-term prospects, and the wider world which awaits him, because you have so little control or influence on its shape and movement.

You know that one day you'll be casting your son into life, like wheat chaff into the breeze, and watch it take him slowly away from your arms. This knowledge makes you want to hold onto the present moments— these first few fleeting days and nights of his new life— that much harder.

You also wonder at what kind of person Mom and Dad, along with the rest of his family and friends, will raise. You know he'll have our physical characteristics. But which ideas, attitudes, hopes, aspirations, and codes of honor will he take on, and which will he reject? Can you give him "the best" of what you have, point him to places beyond where you reached and touched? Or will he inherit your weaknesses and frailties?

As new parents, these thoughts, questions, and speculations come easily and naturally. They must be as much a part of having and raising a baby as are the milk bottle, the diaper pins, the late-night cries, and the adorable expressions. Collectively, as people, similar thoughts, questions, and speculations return to us during this holiday season as we recall the Christmas Story. How was this past year? Did we do "the best" we could? What lies ahead? Can we do better with ourselves, and with our world?

"Fear not," the angel told the shepherds, "for behold, I bring you good tidings of great joy, which shall be to all people."

A child is born. Life continues. Hope, with all of its opportunities and possibilities, is renewed.

A Reunion at a Place Called 'Memories'

Our high school class is meeting this month for its 20th year reunion at a place called "Memories." As one grows older, "Memories" is more and more the preferred place to dwell.

I doubt if very many people can look back over 20 years and not feel the world has changed or, more importantly, that they have. If your vantage point is one of even greater years, then obviously a comparison of two decades would seem less drastic.

Still, for those of us now pushing 40, the differences between then and now— both in the world around us and in that world within us— are seemingly pronounced. We left school at the tail end of the '60s (please, no analogy) in a time of social turmoil. There was the Vietnam War, which for young men was of profound importance. The conflict, rightfully so, dominated much of the public debate and stirred much passion. Also in that context were the civil rights efforts and the ensuing black power movement, the city riots which included Detroit, the assassinations, the student demonstrations at colleges, more openness about sex, choices like grass and LSD, long hair, a war on poverty, and much, much more.

It was a whirlwind of conflicts and clashes, the toppling of established ideas and methods in favor of different ones. There was also the push-and-shove between haves and have-nots, the powerful and the powerless, of the old and the new. Some of what changed or evolved was, and is, good. Some, in retrospect, wasn't. You have roads that you can take, decisions of which direction to head towards. With high ideals and lofty hopes, many in our generation started off on a promising by-way. But, with too many the quest turned inward or became reckless. The wrong forks were taken. Like so many social and cultural clashes, the pendulum swung from one excess or orthodoxy past the point of common ground to another excess or equally rigid doctrine.

I don't think our actual high school days were affected too much by any of this. The cultural and social upheaval was happening elsewhere. We saw it on TV and in the movies, heard about it in our music, and read about it in the newspapers and magazines, but we were mainly bystanders rather than active participants. Some of us were, no doubt, curious about what was happening. A few, as I recall, tugged on the apron strings. But most of us were still hesitant about embracing any of it, reluctant to break out of the boundaries set by parents, the school, and the community's code of acceptable thoughts and behavior. Changes and influences— good or bad— come slowly to small, country towns. However, soon or later, they do eventually arrive.

I think we were bored and restless as was any teenager before or after us, as seemingly confident about our abilities and opinions, and as adept at masking any underlying insecurities. The world, as it always does when you finally reach the age of 17 and 18, seemed big and promising, and easily taken on. It still is big and promising, but after 20 years the world has managed to cut us down to size.

Chaos and conflict still swirl. Now we have concerns about AIDS, and environmental time bombs that are exploding, or will go off one day. There is a drug epidemic and related lawlessness, along with the worry of maintaining our standard of living in a competitive world marketplace. In addition are the emotions over abortion, the effort to hold onto individual liberties in an increasingly technological society, the Middle East wars, a growing gap (both here and abroad) between those who are economically stable and those who are not, and much more. Established ideas and methods are being questioned. The push-and-shove continues.

Each member of our '69 class, in our own way, has found a place in this world, made decisions that took us along paths that (for most) were both wise and ill-advised. Now, with 20 years gone by since high school, having traversed that watershed between childhood and adulthood, we can turn back briefly and, in doing so, take stock in what has occurred around us, and within us. No other judges or juries are needed.

My retrospect?

I wish as teenagers we'd camped a little longer on the hillside, danced a while longer in the moonlight, laughed and enjoyed each other a bit more, hung on longer to the dwindling moments of youth… and been less eager to charge into the fray and do battle with adulthood. Time, though, was not our ally. Having charged forward, eagerly rushing into the grown-up world, positive of our ability to handle the myriad of challenges and responsibilities, it pushed us onward. Now, as we look back, all those days and years have slipped by, and we can only meet again at a place called "Memories."

Pondering the Camping Life

On this still-dark morning, the rain has begun to pour at a steadier pace. In the distance, a rumble of thunder sounds, indicating that the storm is drawing closer. Flashes of lightning have begun to periodically illuminate the yard. They reveal a gothic scene of black twisted tree limbs aglow in a sinister white light.

The spring deluge should melt off the last stubborn traces of snow and begin to wash the dirt and grit off highways, sidewalks, and lawns; nature's warm showers cleaning us off after the long and messy winter.

Inside, protected from the elements, I drink coffee and prepare for the day's task of newspapering. Our bulldog 'Emma' rests a few feet away, gnawing on her chew toy. Normally at this time of the morning, she's camped in Bradley's room, keeping vigil beside his bed as he enjoys a final couple hours of slumber. But Bradley spent the night elsewhere, so 'Emma' makes do with her pal's old man. She abandons the toy and starts to chew on a section of the Sunday paper. I scold her. I'm unsure if this is a symptom of canine depravity or normalcy, but it seems hardly appropriate for the dog to be treating a newspaper (that citadel of democracy) with such nonchalance.

The day before, after scanning the Sunday paper for timely information and entertainment possibilities, we visited a nearby RV show and looked at the assorted models. They ranged from the grandiose (at least for our household budget) to the austere. The latter captured my attention. It was a small pop-up camper, the lowest priced unit on the show floor; one step up the evolutionary ladder from a large tent.

Back in the salad days of youth, I'd join the Zdans and company on their regular camping excursions at the state park in Interlochen with hardly more than the sleeping bag on my back. We'd joke about the fancy rigs that surrounded us. Part of our entertainment, back then, was to sit in our chairs, a refreshment in hand, and watch a newly-arrived camper attempt to back his long trailer through the narrow gap of trees onto the site. The luxury sedan that towed it (like the trailer) was seemingly out-of-place in the north woods. To assist him in the effort, his wife would be outside, shouting directions and warnings. Pretty soon the man would be yelling at his mate, blaming her hand waving for his inability to complete the job quickly.

Once parked, the couple, plus any children, would set up camp, plug the electrical line into the outlet, and disappear back into the unit. At night they'd venture out-of-doors, place the portable TV on the table, apparently get bitten by a mosquito, and retreat (with the television) back inside. "Why don't they just camp in their backyards and save themselves the gas?" I'd wonder.

Ah, the cruelty of youth.

Now, as an aging baby-boomer, I wander amid the RVs, admire their home-away-from-home conveniences, test out the comforts, and daydream about relaxing in a lounge chair under the shade of the awning, and watching the ball game on a lazy August afternoon. Leave the tents, the nights on the hard ground, the damp sleeping bags, and the cold mornings to the younger set. I've been there, and done that. But now I'm here, ready for a softer approach.

Bradley, although only five, is a veteran of the camping scene—the modern, comfortable kind, that is. His grandparents own a nice motor home and have taken him on several outings. He sleeps in the bunk over the driver's cab and knows all the ins-and-outs of organizing a weekend outing. A pop-up model would be a step down on the luxury scale from the level he's used to; still the thought of camping (in and of itself) excites him. His enthusiasm is contagious. We hadn't actually come to the show to buy anything, just to look. Suddenly, we're signing a purchase agreement. The sales lady beams. She wants to hire Bradley for other selling jobs, seeing how easily he swayed his Mom and Dad.

Later that night he questions me at length about the situation, a relentless prosecutor on the trail of evidence. I describe how we'll set up the camper, and what we can do: cook our meals, store equipment, sit at the table for our meals or use it to play cards when it rains, turn on the heater if it's too chilly, and sleep on a soft mattress. I suggest that we bring the dome tent for changing out of wet swimsuits, and hopefully track less sand into the pop-up.

I also list all of the recreational alternatives that await us. Besides swimming and card playing, there'll be biking, fishing, and boating. Of course, camping is not all fun. I mention the necessary jobs we'll have to perform like cranking up the roof, pulling out the two slide-outs and bracing them (those slide-outs will be where we sleep), putting in the screen door, hooking up the gas stove, plugging in the electrical cord, pulling out the awning, getting a picnic table, and unpacking all the utensils and other equipment.

Having listened intently, he then repeats part of this information back to me. After a minute or so, he stops and says, "Now it's your turn to talk." I'm not used to someone wanting me to gab on and on, let alone repeat myself. I try not to abuse the opportunity.

I talk again about swimming in the lake, walking in the woods, going to the park restroom to shower, fixing breakfast, and sitting around the camp fire. The list is exhausting. This is the stuff of wide-eyed adventure to Bradley. And movement.

I add that one of the enjoyments of camping is resting; of sitting or reclining and, while doing so, reading, or better yet, taking a nap. He's less excited about this mental picture that's being drawn. He doesn't say much, but he's probably thinking… "If that's what we're going to do, we might as well stay in our backyard and save the gas."

Kicking Up Some Dust

On Monday mornings, if there's been little precipitation to dampen the ground, the dust flies as we drive along the graveled roads of southern Iosco Township. Our task is to deliver the weekly newspaper to residences here. Grandpa Lloyd, riding shotgun, handles those on the right side, while I take care of those on the left.

Our politics are probably somewhat similar, although you can never be sure with my grandfather. He's by all definitions "Independent." I hope I am, too.

The dust is the most visible sign of our presence. We kick some up as we pass through the countryside each week, although it settles down soon enough, and then everything goes back to normal— until the next motorist comes along. I suppose there's an analogy there for life itself— our individual ones, that is.

The dust is now settling from last week's November General election. Those public servants selected, the propositions decided on; they all have direct and indirect impacts on us. But maybe not nearly as much significance as we might assume. Our own actions and inactions are perhaps more telling over the long haul.

The partisans warn us of doom-and-gloom if the other guy or gal is elected, or if a given proposal passes or fails. The prediction is usually more the negative possibility (or worst-case scenario) than what positive benefit will come about if their candidate or position meets with voter approval.

Putting out a weekly newspaper seems of small consequence compared to this grander scheme of things, namely of a presidential election. A young George Adams arrived in Fowlerville at the end of Grant's administration back in 1874. He and a partner began publishing a "four-pager." He soon became the sole proprietor. Since then, there's been a paper with local news and information showing up on a regular basis. We're just part of this long chain.

The debut of Adam's weekly publication came three years after a rail line was constructed on the south edge of the village, the railroad then being the chief and most efficient means of transporting goods and services beyond the confines of a small community located in Michigan's interior. It also served to more frequently co-mingle people and ideas, ending a more isolated existence.

The first white settlers had arrived here in the mid-1830s. Their main transportation link had been the rutted wagon road known as the Grand River Trail, then later "improved" as a plank road. With the completion of this rail line between Detroit and Lansing, with Fowlerville on the route, they would witness a surge in growth and development, and all the ensuing changes those forces bring.

We're presently in the midst of another surge, this one brought on by the relocation of residents from the ring of suburbs that border Detroit, outward into the surrounding Southeastern Michigan countryside. The new homes that dot southern Iosco Township and elsewhere, plus the growing annual enrollment at our local schools, are physical evidence of this occurrence. New people back in the 1870s brought different backgrounds, outlooks, and viewpoints. The same is true now. Old means and methods give way to the pressure of an evolving community.

Nothing is ever fixed and solid, although it may seem so from the vantage point of on-going routines; a slow pace that on occasion might seem stationary. People with their actions and reactions, conceptions and misconceptions, ideas (or lack thereof) mirror the fluidity of greater Nature. The process is that of continuous arranging and rearranging, of ebb and flow, of expansion and retraction.

George Adams published his area weekly for 55 years. His overriding moral passion was Prohibition: the banning of alcohol as a legal beverage. Prohibition was enacted into Constitutional law in 1920, culminating a long crusade by its supporters. He must have felt elated by his role in this accomplishment. He died in 1930, a year after he had sold his publication and printing business and retired. In 1933 Prohibition was repealed.

Great issues, heated debates, Presidential campaigns… the emotions aroused by them, and the hopes and fears they inspire, are nothing new on the American scene. The forces and consequences of change and differing believe are part of our daily bread.

But oftentimes we get too preoccupied with the "big picture," and with an unquenchable thirst of anticipation. We're looking beyond the moment, wondering what momentous event the next hour or day might bring. By doing so, we can miss the small pleasures of here-and-now. We can miss the importance of friendly conversation, an old story retold, a funny joke, the cornfields and hay fields, the wood lots and swamps, the folks waving as we leave them a paper, the cows indifferent to it all, and the squirrels fleeing to the safety of nearby trees.

The words are written, the speeches have been given, the points of contention debated. People have read them, or listened, or joined the fray. But eventually the hoopla of the campaign fades away. Time goes on to other concerns and situations. You go along until one day it's all gotten too far ahead. Then you look back, and see the dust settling.

My grandfather, in one of his many moments of humor, recites a poem as we deliver the papers. "I had to memorize this back in country school," he explains. It goes:

The owl was perched in the oak.
The more he heard, the less he spoke.
The less he spoke, the more he heard.
Don't you wish more people were like that wise old bird?

We have each other. These moments and this place. Enjoy them.

The "New Electric Pencil Sharpener Arrives"

My son Bradley, a first grader, roused me from a much-deserved afternoon nap the other day. Not an unusual occurrence, by the way. I suspect he prides himself in such mischief. But on this day he had an added motivation.

"Look what I got from the store," he announced loudly from the foot of the bed, and pulled a small box from a bag.

I squinted from still sleepy eyes. "It's my new electric pencil sharpener," he added, possibly aware that I can't see too far these days without my spectacles.

Bradley left and went next door to his room. As I sought to drift back to sleep, I began hearing the soft hum of grinding pencil wood. He yelled for his mom to come look. Being a good mother, she marveled at the sharpened pencils, then asked, "How long do you keep a pencil in?"

"As long as you want," he answered.

Several minutes later he showed back up beside me. "Got any pencils that need sharpening?" he wondered.

"I'll check," I replied, giving up all pretense of slumber. "How's it going?"

"I'm giving it a rest so it won't break," he said, and added, "It's a nice one, just like my teacher's. There was another one in the store that ran on batteries, but I wanted this one. Now you won't have to sharpen my pencils downstairs. I can do it myself."

His reference was to an old hand-operated sharpener I have mounted on a wall, above a high storage cabinet, in the basement. I obtained it long ago from my grandmother, a school teacher, who had kept it for years in the back room of her farm home. A metallic-gray steel contraption, its color had dulled with age and a bit of rust had formed around the edges. But despite its signs of age, this sharpener still does the job, when needed.

I just don't need to "do the job" that often. Disposable ink pens, the electronic typewriter, and an adding machine perform most of my writing and figuring. However, the pencil (with eraser) is not an obsolete tool for young students. Bradley had recently asked me to sharpen a few of his pencils, then watched as I reached over the tall cabinet and cranked the handle. Apparently having witnessed this old mechanical device, and having seen his teacher's electric gadget, he opted, as so many have before him, for the labor-saving and speedier convenience.

I wasn't completely surprised by the purchase. He'd mentioned his desire for one the day before. But he often possesses such impulses— fueled usually by television commercials. I claim poverty, or resort to a firm "no," and begin fending off the steady "Why nots?". With this acquisition, however, he planned to use his own money— accumulated from recent grandparent gifts. Besides, a school-related purchase seemed difficult to discourage. Hopefully, the electric pencil sharpener will last as long as the mechanical one. Bradley will need to practice a lot of penmanship, drawing, and arithmetic to keep it in use, unless he just keeps grinding down pencils for the heck of it. In that case he'll soon be soliciting new pencils.

Out of curiosity, I check the hand-cranked unit. The attached factory label indicates it's an 'Apsco Giant 51' with offices in Beverly Hills, Calif. and Rockford, Ill. Lord knows what long-ago year it was manufactured. On one end is a circular cover with six different hole sizes. You can turn the cover, adjusting it to get the exact diameter you want. I failed to realize pencils came in such a variety of widths — or did so once upon a time.

Bradley's new model, on the other hand, offers only one hole. So, once again, modern technology has deprived the consumer a choice, in favor of expediency and uniformity.

Local Participation Key to Self-Government

Every so often an issue surfaces that riles up a number of our townspeople. They organize among themselves, then arrive *en masse* at the village council meeting. Tempers surge at high pitch. Council trustees, used to dealing with one or two disgruntled citizens at a time, appear tense and uncomfortable. The audience, sensing that unease, and getting a little giddy with the power of numbers, lists its grievances or outlines its objections, and demands a favorable action.

In the beginning, calmer heads try to prevail. A couple of folks in the crowd actually realize there's other possible sides to the issue, and that discussion of these contrasting views is a prelude in the decision-making process. A council trustee will invariably explain that he or she represents all of the town residents and has to also weigh the general interest. The utterance is usually greeted with loud grumbles and sarcastic comments, and you get a real sense of how a lynch mob evolves.

The only humor is when a member of the audience threatens political retaliation; vowing to "vote the trustees out of office" should they be presumptuous enough to decide against the crowd's wishes. No one on the council chuckles, though. That comes later (more like a nervous laugh actually), after this segment of the meeting has mercifully ended. The officials wait until after the public has headed off to their respective homes, and a few items of regular council business have been covered which helps calm the mental jitters. Then, during a short recess, they sip on their Styrofoam cups of coffee and go over the highlights of the confrontation, including the threat of retaliation.

First of all, they're volunteers, not career politicians. Voting them out of office would probably be more a favor than a blow. Their egos might suffer, but otherwise their various lives will go happily on. But the ballot-box threat is pretty much an idle one. Hardly anyone votes in the annual municipal elections held each winter. The last exercise of democracy saw 200 out of over 1,500 registered residents trouble themselves by showing up to the polls— a normal turnout. Sometimes, if there's a hotly-contested race the numbers might push up a bit higher. Otherwise, apathy is the normal response.

That means most of the people at the meeting haven't voted, and, if old habits repeat, which they generally do, they'll continue to avoid the effort. Were the election held that night or within a week or so, they might. But emotion— the high pitch of anger and frustration— is seldom long-lasting. They simmer down, and most of those in attendance will shrug their shoulders and mutter "why bother?"

Too many confuse this smoke with the real fire of grass roots government. The shouts, threats, ultimatums, and red faces go with the territory. Nevertheless, the hard work of democracy necessitates knowledge of the ongoing issue. It requires voting, lending ideas and possibilities to the decision making, serving on advisory boards, and running for local office. You won't always get a pat on the back for the time and trouble. More likely it'll instead be a kick, and aimed a bit lower.

Yet this effort and consistency of involvement will have more influence in the long run than those occasional flashes of loud shouts and much temper. True, the flashes may alter immediate direction and change minds. However, more often than not, the course and minds revert to previously held positions.

Debates on state and national issues, unfortunately, evoke more storm than calm persuasion. We seemingly lurch from crisis to crisis, from boiling pot to boiling pot. One week this group screams, while the next week another has the spotlight. Citizens dial the radio talk host to vent their spleen or, marching lock-step to the phone, dial the 800 number that their favorite TV preacher has offered for pressure purposes. Some of them call direct to their Congressperson's office to register their immediate dissatisfaction. Others send financial support to special-interest lobbyists to plead their special concern.

None of this is wrong. In fact, this sort of reaction is preferable to indifference. Still, these choices are an easy way around the hard work. Bursts of passion are allowed to substitute for intellectual engagement; impatience pushes aside deliberation. At the state and national levels such responses make you a number, a part of the percentage of *for* or *against*. Otherwise, there's little opportunity to detail your beliefs and thoughts, to test them in discussion and debate, and to help hammer them into policies and governmental direction.

That sort of engagement and impact is offered (for most of us) only at the local level— at meetings of town councils, school boards, township and county boards, planning and zoning commissions as well as at public hearings, meet-the-candidate nights, legislative coffees, and issue forums. It is an involvement that is enhanced by reading, thoughtful consideration, listening, conversation, and a willingness to consider other points of view and work towards compromise and consensus.

Maybe none of this is as much fun as shaking a fist, or as intoxicating as tossing the symbolic rope over the branch, but it seems a better means of democratic self-rule.

Christmas Returns

It's beginning to look a lot like Christmas. The other day we put up the artificial tree; a holiday adornment we've now owned for several years. We abandoned the natural variety after we installed a new living room carpet. Damage from leaking water was a concern, but mostly my wife no longer wished to pick up fallen pine needles.

We'd planned to buy a new (artificial) tree this year, since the current one looked a little ragged. The nearby shopping center advertised several "on sale" models before Thanksgiving. We zipped right over to the store, studied the various floor samples, and picked out a tree we thought appeared the most life-like. Our choice was a replica of a Douglas Fir. The man-made needles resembled the "Real McCoys," and we knew, unlike the natural ones, that they'd stay put when the tree came down after the New Year's festivities.

But this model was not to be found amid the boxes underneath the table display. We located a sales clerk. "All out," she answered after also searching the rows of boxed trees, confirming our own suspicion. We felt disappointment. Either this specimen proved a popular choice and had already sold out, or, more likely, the ordering people failed to realize its appeal and obtained too few to meet demand. "You can get a rain check," the clerk advised.

We did. And waited over a week. But the check— in this case the Douglas Fir— is still "in the mail." Finally, we could no longer stall our six-year-old son who's wanted to decorate a tree since early November— his requests beginning at the same time the TV cartoon advertisements launched their holiday marketing. Since I lacked the appetite to travel from store-to-store in hopes of finding an adequate (and affordable) substitute, the most feasible alternative was to get the (by now) family heirloom out of the basement closet, and assemble it one more time.

I hadn't noticed before, but the name on the box stated that this was a Northeast Fir. Egad, we're such traditionalists. The tree did indeed look a bit worse for wear standing there without its covering. Heck, so do I. After four strands of lights, dozens of ornaments (several of them saying "Baby's First Christmas"), and a few lines of beads and miniature gift boxes were all in place, the old bush looked pretty good.

The rest of the room was then decorated with our holiday keepsakes. These included the nativity scene on the fireplace mantel, with Bradley's stocking hung underneath it; the ceramic Victorian carolers and church arranged on an end table, plus a crocheted wall hanging of Santa located next to the door. On another table were displayed the assorted knick knacks: a wicker sleigh and reindeer, a wooden Santa along with wooden Christmas trees, an angel, and a pair of candles.

Earlier we had put colored lights on the magnolia shrub in the front yard and had hung two small evergreen wreaths on either side of the garage door. By the day's end— with Bradley supervising most of the operation— a spot was found for all of the strands of lights, each knick knack, and every ornament that had been boxed the year before. Some broken bulbs were tossed out; however, these had already been replaced with new items purchased at a bazaar.

There are folks who go for a specific theme when decking their halls, or who have an attractive, well-pondered color scheme in mind. I marvel at the energy, and imagination required for such picturesque, even breathtaking displays. On my part there's little desire to emulate. What we do is arrange all of these past possessions (along with a few recent acquisitions) as that day's mood and happenstance dictate. The result looks pretty similar from the December before, yet there's no deliberate pattern, no preconceived diagram. The color scheme is like Dolly Parton's coat of many colors.

That evening the lights twinkle in the dark room— the blues, greens, reds, and yellows resembling tiny candles. The hanging bulbs sparkle from their reflected glow. "Baby's First Christmas" and now a little boy's sixth. It wasn't so long ago when I was that youngster.

Christmas returns, bringing recollections of bygone holidays. They are as much heirlooms as the special ornaments. We un-wrap them each holiday, and re-decorate the mind. With these cherished memories in mind, we go forth to celebrate the season, adding new experiences to the array of all those previous ones.

Frankenmuth Visited: Family Fun Center

Frankenmuth. Located alongside the Cass River in Saginaw County, the town serves as a trading center for surrounding agriculture. But the place is more famous as Michigan's Little Bavaria, home of chicken dinners, year-round Christmas, and German-style beers and sausages.

Day visitors— people driving here for a meal and shopping— make the locale a leading tourism destination. A nearby outlet shopping mall in Birch Run (just off US-23) adds to the lure. With the availability of overnight accommodations, the visit can be extended, and one recent Sunday-thru-Tuesday we added to the numbers by taking a mini-vacation at the Bavarian Inn Lodge. The hotel advertises itself as a "Conference Center and Family Fun Center." The former was probably a major consideration in the initial planning. That, plus the idea of catering to older, childless couples seeking ambiance. But it's the families— mom and dad with younger kids— who now appear to be the bread-and-butter trade.

We fit quite comfortably into the latter marketing niche. Along with the other families, we had access to two indoor pools (one shallow for very young children), adjacent hot tubs, video and pinball games, air hockey, pool tables, a two-story Bavarian Village built at children's scale, a snack bar, a rathskeller, a restaurant, a lounge, an exercise room, and a gift shop. Such all-inclusive lodging is not unique to this place. One-stop convenience is as widespread now for leisure and vacations as it is for shopping.

The kids pool is humbling, yet reassuring. Most of the couples here, keeping an eye on their children, are in their thirties. Slightly protruding bellies and "love handles" are the norm, unlike the summer beaches where the lithe forms of the teenagers dominate. My own shape seems worse than most, partly from being slightly older, and therefore having more time to deteriorate, but mainly from extra helpings, neglected exercises, and the desk-bound career. "Next year I'll be in better shape," I vow to myself, a repeat of the pledge made the year before when we stayed here.

While the kids splash around the pool, the adults gravitate to the warm, vibrating waters of the hot tub. There's the physical relaxation, along with the mental sense (real, or maybe only imagined) that we're unwinding. Stress and job burnout have become the great bogey men of my generation. Self-help articles proliferate. So-called cures abound, including the hot tub and its cousin, the whirlpool.

A carefully observed separation between job and home life, interesting hobbies, less obsession on money and status might have a more lasting effect. That approach, plus a better understanding of both personal goals and expectations, and accepting some limitations, would (I suspect) do much to relieve the tenseness, frustrations, and fatigue apparently inherent in much work and routine activity. However, as a culture, we like easy answers and quick fixes, admire motion and tangible success, and the hot tub does offer a nice place to sit and soothe.

The TV in our room offers a cable menu of 40 channels. The viewing frenzy begins. I lie on the bed and flip through them, pausing only occasionally to briefly watch some interesting tidbit. I have a hard time sticking with any program, fearing a better, more interesting one might be broadcasting somewhere else.

At home we've forgone this modern indulgence (for now), relying on the small selection of VHS and UHF stations in our area. Some temptations are too great and must be kept at arm's length.

Another mindless frenzy takes place on our first night in Frankenmuth. We go over to the Bavarian Inn Restaurant, across the river from the Lodge, for the obligatory chicken dinner. As always, it's a feast of dark and white meat, dressing, mashed potatoes, cole slaw, cranberry relish, squash, chicken noodle soup, cottage cheese, bread, jam, and ice cream.

Later, as we browse the shops in the basement, I pick up a fact sheet of how much food is sold annually. During this latest year, the staff served over 700,000 pounds of poultry, which came from approximately 205,500 chickens. Other meats and seafood amount to just over 170,000 pounds. They also sold over a million cups of coffee.

We dine at Zehnder's Restaurant— the town's other renowned eatery— the next day. The German motif, so pronounced at the Bavarian Inn and elsewhere in town, is low key at this establishment. But chicken and the hearty appetite are still king. I order a plate of fried chicken livers, and am amply rewarded.

Bronner's CHRISTmas Store is the other star in Frankenmuth's constellation. Located in spacious quarters, the yuletide season is a year-around business for this local firm. Hundreds and hundreds of holiday ornaments, decorations, trims, books, music tapes, artificial trees, nativity scenes, knick knacks, cups, wall hangings, and possible gifts line the walls, hang from the ceiling, and make up merchandise islands.

Clients come from all over the state, the nation, and the world. They range from individual customers to bus tours to buyers for large municipalities. Many celebrities have also stopped in for a visit; their presence commemorated with a photograph. They are usually posed next to a member of the Bronner family, and these pictures are hung throughout the store. Our last two Michigan governors— Jim Blanchard and John Engler— are prominently displayed, along with several stars from the *Lawrence Welk Show*, and other well-known personalities from entertainment, government, religion and the news media. The CHRISTmas Store has obviously been spotlighted in numerous newspaper, magazine, radio and TV features over the years, and these, too, are highlighted; the articles suitably framed and the broadcasts remembered with ("yes") a photograph. No one rushes over with a camera to record my presence, testament to my relative obscurity. "There are virtues to being unknown," I mentally console myself as I move away from this wall of fame.

Early morning, on both days of our stay, I go downstairs to the Franconian Restaurant for coffee. A group of ministers has been holding a conference, and each time I've been seated near several of them as they eat breakfast and visit.

One fellow seems determined to comment on everything. There are about a dozen others at the table, and he handles about half the talking. His voice projects, an asset when giving sermons to the congregation, however of dubious value in the Franconian. Whenever a handful of males gather— whether it's drinkers in a bar, business associates, boys on the playground, newspaper hacks, or even men of the cloth— one or two of them attempt(s) to dazzle. This may be due to their personality type, sense of insecurity, aggressive intention, or poor manners.

Having been guilty of this conduct from time to time, I'm quick to spot it in others. I try not to be overly condemning. Let some other fellow cast the first stone. The overheard conversations are a bit jarring, though. I'm used to sipping my morning coffee in the quiet solitude of home, undisturbed, my wife and son still slumbering. All of this early talk and activity is disconcerting. Normally, the early morning is the only languid moment of my day. From there, I'm generally off on a trot and, on occasion, even a gallop. While a vacation offers a break from the day-to-day, the transition can be difficult.

Because most of us are so busy moving and doing, we forget how to "turn it down a few notches" and make our respective lives slower and nearly boring; necessary components (it seems to me) to any tranquility, relaxation, and renewal. Like so much else in life, perhaps we try too hard, even when on vacation. I guess there's an art to "taking it easy." Like a lot of things, I could stand more practice.

Wide Awake & Thinking

A full night's sleep has eluded me lately. No, not from having a guilty conscience— at least not one of which I'm aware. Besides, such sleep disruption (from that cause) is usually short-lived; the human mind being quite adept at forgiving its shortcomings. Nor is the trouble from digestive difficulties, like eating spicy pizza just before bedtime, then awakening a few hours later with heartburn and an unquenchable thirst.

My slumber is interrupted by a hamster named Teddy. My young son acquired the little critter as a pet, along with a cage. Inside this hamster's cubicle sets a spinning wheel. Animal behaviorists or other such experts apparently discovered that these fellows— once on this circular treadmill— scamper forward, causing the wheel to continuously turn until they tire of the effort. Certainly, it's a splendid idea to get the animal to do this, providing the pet with vigorous exercise in what's otherwise cramped quarters.

I can attest that hamsters— or Teddy at least— possess amazing stamina, able to operate this spinning wheel for what seems a great length of time. While unable to precisely correlate the hamster's accomplishment to a human scale, I will speculate that the feat is equivalent to a long, brisk jog. Since, at best, I'm only up to a long, brisk walk, Teddy's got me beat as a physical fitness buff.

The problem is that hamsters are nocturnal by nature, and the wheel emits an audible noise while spinning. When Teddy, at around two or three o'clock in the morning, decides to climb up into his exercise machine and go lickety-split, the ensuing hum arouses me from my sweet dreams. The hamster and his cage are, I should note, located in Bradley's room. However, our sleeping quarters are next to his, and our humble middle-class accommodations are not completely sound proof.

This recurring situation has provided me with unexpected time to think. Most of us have too few opportunities for this unhurried endeavor. When arising in the morning— or whenever we begin our respective daily cycle— there awaits the hurry and scurry of routine. Distractions abound, including numerous ongoing interactions with family members, co-workers, friends and neighbors, and others who cross our path, and prompt an exchange of words. Maybe some of us employ those few moments (while savoring the wake-up beverage or during the commute to and from work) to consider the intricacies of life, and our place here amid the stars. Normally, though, we're just too busy or, ironically, have a lot on our mind.

Deep thinking gets a lot of praise, and rightly so. Still there's a time and place. Like when you're fishing. Or maybe when you're celebrating a notable anniversary, and stare at the wall, wondering where all the years have gone? Wide-eyed in the middle of the night may be tolerable on occasion, even though most of us hate the situation, knowing full well that we'll be pooped the next day. As far as having our sleep disturbed for several nights, well, that's an entirely different matter. I can be entertained by my thoughts as much as the next guy, journeying to the seldom-visited recesses of the mind. But I like sleeping better.

Being awakened the other night by Teddy, I tossed and turned, finally got up, had a glass of milk, and returned to bed. I then got to contemplating journalism— this chosen career of mine. What I do, and what the hamster does, are somewhat similar, I decide. Journalists pursue this ambiguous thing we call "news," unknown by most people until made known by us. The news, initially, is often a chaos of facts and impressions until organized into a digestible form. We offer the events (or series of events) to the reader, and then, shortly after publication, this particular news ceases its freshness and immediacy, and becomes history.

Each work day we climb into the wheel, go round and round, and get off. News is offered, becomes the past, and we start all over again. Not all news is momentary. It can be a slice-of-life account or a summary of ongoing events or existing conditions. News can also be episodic: the sequential reports unfolding over a period of time. Examples would be a court trial or a war. Eventually, though, an ending arrives, and reporter and readers move onto the next piece of news.

That's not to suggest journalism is futile. Far from it. The point of this analogy is not that I'm going round and round in a circle to nowhere, but that the effort involves a great deal of repetition; and it's good exercise to climb onto the wheel and start moving.

The hamster's nightly job on the treadmill might seem without much purpose or merit to us. He doesn't really go anywhere, yet this activity is part of what the hamster "is." By comparison, if a more sophisticated being, someone with higher intelligence, happened to observe our human activities, it likewise might question the purpose and ultimate value. But work, routine, and day-to-day repetitions with family, friends, and associates are what a human "is."

We have the measuring stick— both tangible and intangible— called "progress," or "improvements." As individuals we are born and grow up. Some of us have children and attempt to raise them; we grow old and pass away. All the while we're conducting some form of reoccurring routine (a cycle if you will) as part of a family, a community and this species. While doing so, we feel, with justification, that there's a lineal movement as well; that what we do (most of us anyway) contributes to the betterment of others as well as ourselves. The accumulated efforts of each, we reason, cause the forward movement of all.

A Mouse and a Cat… In the House

A mouse has spent this long winter in our humble abode. He resides in the space between the basement ceiling and the upstairs floor. The previous owners of our ranch-style home finished off the basement with wall panels, carpet, and fiber-wood ceiling tiles, with the tiles being stapled to the bottom of the floor joists.

This finished-off downstairs was a great selling point when we purchased the place, and it remains an asset. But this overhead space is sealed off— akin to a secret passageway in an English manor— inaccessible to humans unless the tiles are torn off. This mouse, having discovered an outside entry portal, currently roams this part of our residence without immediate threat, since I'm opposed to ruining the ceiling.

I hear the telltale scurrying of his feet along the tiles in the morning, after I come down to drink coffee, and plot the day's agenda. So far I've not noticed any signs of mouse activity elsewhere in our living quarters, allowing me to set a trap. We've had an occasional mouse get inside before, and I eventually disposed of them with the traditional method of a cheese bait and spring trap.

Those mice were more secretive and silent; spotted only as they scampered along a wall from one area of cover to another, or by their droppings. The current intruder is downright noisy; unaware of my lurking presence only a couple yards below his runway. I'm annoyed by this boldness. Were the fellow quieter, I'd probably think less about him and how best to deal with this intrusion. I certainly wouldn't be writing about him. Were he softer afoot in his movements, I might even ignore him. No sound, no problem. But the morning jogs above me preclude such convenient recourse. I'm reminded each time I hear him that as a husband, father, and good citizen, I hold a duty. A mouse is not allowed in the house.

Cats, on the other hand, are given that privilege; at least by many people, our family now among them. The kitten that Bradley and his mother brought home last summer— not yet matured to a young lady — has enjoyed free wandering rights.

Like me, the cat is baffled about what to do with the impudent mouse. Each morning Kristy (my son's name for his pet) accompanies me to the basement. Hearing the noise above her, Kristy leaps from desk to dresser to bookcase trying to follow the moving sound. She cocks her head once it stops, attempting (I assume) to catch any further stirring which would pinpoint the trespasser's exact whereabouts.

I doubt Kristy knows she's hearing a mouse running, unless a cat's instincts do indeed tell it that this scurrying noise indicates a special meal; a meal her ancestors have relished over the long centuries. More likely the innate curiosity of the feline is triggered. She simply wants to find out what's going on; her inquisitive nature shared by town gossips and many journalists. Should she actually spot the critter out in the open, then she might take the matter into her own paws. And, were she to accomplish this feat, I could avoid having to one day bait the trap, and worry about accidentally catching my finger in it as I set the spring.

While Kristy operates on instinct (including inquisitiveness), I rely on accumulated knowledge and a moderately-developed faculty of reason. These are the main weapons I bring to the task of mouse removal. I possess curiosity. However, in this matter of the mouse I mainly wonder where the entry hole is located. If I find it, then I could plug up the opening and avoid future annoyance. Then I could do my daily plotting and coffee drinking without distraction.

I'm aware an inconsistency of sorts exists here. The mouse— other than its brief romps— has so far avoided contact with the rest of my life. For all practical purposes, he's had little more impact than a bird flying by our window. I see the bird, perhaps watch its flight, and have soon forgotten it. Yet I hear the mouse, and wish its departure.

The cat is another matter. Kristy's presence is quite evident. I'm reminded of her when I find strands of her hair on my dress slacks, when she jumps onto my lap while I'm reading the paper, or when she plays with Bradley (which results in more racket than a herd of mice). Other signs include the aroma of the litter box, her habit of resting on my easy chair just when I'm ready to use it, and meowing outside our bedroom door at three o'clock in the morning.

Sometimes she's an amusement. Other times a bit of a bother. Mostly she just goes about her business, and I go about mine.

No matter. We've cut a deal with Kristy— the same one millions of other humans (in the past and today) have made with their pets. As the family house cat, she gets to share the joint with us, being regarded as part of the clan. We expect, in turn, that she use the litter box, also not climb on the kitchen counters or dinner table (not when we're around any way), and at some point – Please! – quit waking us up so early.

We've cut no such deals with the mouse.

On Writing

I shall begin by confessing that I'm a newspaperman. The small town variety, who nowadays goes by the handle of "community journalist." But whether you practice the trade before the hometown folks as I do, or on a larger scale, the basic means of conveyance should be similar. As a norm, the delivery is done in the detached voice of the third-person reporter, with the story told in a recognizable reportorial style.

I've been in this line of work for over 20 years, so I'm accustomed to that familiar third-person distance and format. But a journalist, along with bringing forth those detached news reports, can — under the proper labeling— utilize the additional avenues of opinion, commentary, analysis, and personal experience. In the newspaper trade, such writings are generally called columns or an op-ed pieces and, in the greater world, fall under the heading of an essay. The column or essay allows, if the writer so chooses, a closer proximity with the reader. It allows a means for stepping outside the bounds, within reason, of the news-story format.

I've penned several dozen of these newspaper columns or journalistic and personal essays over the past two decades; the effort satisfying an internal desire to express myself beyond the constraints of the straight news account. That's hardly a unique characteristic among reporters, or for that matter the larger public.

I've come to enjoy the essay. Mainly, I suppose, because this style of writing offers a great deal of latitude. The format allows you to express (as best you can) the point you're trying to get across, or to create a certain effect or mood. In doing this, you can use whatever delivery you're most comfortable with, or believe would be most appropriate and convincing. In addition, you can include any other odds and ends you feel like… all of these options (and more) are at your disposal as you sit down at your desk.

An essay can range from a scholarly, structured, focused examination of an issue, topic, or bone of contention— a piece in an academic journal or an article in *the New York Review of Books*, for example— to the informal, rambling, personal chit-chat of a letter from one friend to another. In that expanse of possibilities and choices, there is excitement as well as challenge. The late E.B. White, in the Foreword of his 1977 collection called *Essays*, stated: "The essayist is a self-liberated man, sustained by the childish belief that everything he thinks about, everything that happens to him is of general interest."

White added a few sentences later, "The essayist arises in the morning and, if he has work to do, selects his garb from an unusually extensive wardrobe: he can pull on any sort of shirt, be any sort of person, according to his mood or subject matter— philosopher, scold, jester, raconteur, confidant, pundit, devil's advocate, enthusiast."

Yet, while the options are many and varied, the essential process remains that of observation and reflection. At times, the practitioner might lean more toward one or the other, but more often it's a combination.

An essay, wrote Gore Vidal in the Preface of his 1990 collection *At Home*, derives from the French word *essai*, meaning *an attempt*. "It is simply that," he added, "an attempt to order one's impressions and reflect on a given subject." The judgment of the reader is how well you observe and explain; how informative, interesting, insightful, convincing, engrossing, and, yes, entertaining your written excursion is.

Like others, I write from interest, curiosity, and concern; using my background, current events, happenstance, and other such props. While we live in an age of increasing specialization, I carry the banner of "generalist." There is much to be admired about the pursuit and accomplishment of expertise and masterly competence. The world is often an easier and more understandable place because of such labor and attainment— the triumph of precision within a given field of endeavor or discipline of study.

Still, there is need, too, for considering the colorful array of bits and pieces, the many potential and plausible patterns, the broad scope, and the multitude of life's trifles. As a writer I like such variety and suffer from mental wanderlust. I suppose I'm like an old hound dog, romping aimlessly about the countryside, sniffing here and there, cocking his head to discern an unusual sound, and then leaving his mark on a tree or bush to make others aware of his recent presence.

***

When reporting on (or simply pondering about) an event, person, locale, issue, or situation; when expressing a concern, belief, or opinion; when touching on a private matter; when looking either ahead or around, or going back into memory; when offering observations and reflections… you can confront both vanity and doubt.

To cobble together an essay undeniably involves a little ego, a conceit that your effort holds merit and worth, and should become part of the community marketplace and public dialogue. Yet, at other moments, there arises the hesitation of doubt; the questioning of 'why' you seek to palm yourself off on an unsuspecting reading audience. There arises the hint of panic as you think about striding out onto the stage, all alone in the spotlight, exposed to the glare of others' scrutiny. You fear your performance will be ridiculed or, worse yet, greeted with indifference.

Too much vanity can be a danger. There's a tendency of making self-righteous and pompous discourses. Regular self-questioning seems advisable. On the other hand, too much pause, uncertainty, and lack of confidence can be equally hazardous. At some point— as in so many of life's ambitions—you need to decide whether to step out onto the stage and take your chances, or remain in the obscurity of the wings. So, between these two extremes, between a cocky attitude and self-doubt, you seek to navigate your passage of written exploration.

Ford Madox Ford mentioned the taletellers "who sit, as it were, by the stoves and are driven by the necessities of their lives to express themselves in such a way as to engross the attention of their hearers… Art is nothing more or less than the faculty, conscious or unconscious, of engrossing the attention of passersby."

Ford, in this instance, was referring to a certain kind of novelist, but I think the analysis is equally true of the entire undertaking. When writing, you're seeking a spot by that stove, a place to inform, clarify, entertain, and influence. For some practitioners, there exists an inner compulsion. With others, it's an outward aspiration. There may be high-minded goals at play, or less flattering ones. A small number possess an inherent talent that makes the act, and outcome, as soaring and seemingly effortless as a bird's flight. As for the rest, it's an acquired craft, a continuous and toilsome apprenticeship.

Whatever the reasons, underlying motives, or causes, whatever the desired results and anticipated rewards, each writer eventually faces the finished piece, decides to quit fretting and tinkering, and lets it go. At that instant the desire is for someone else to read it, and react. The great hope— perhaps vain and yet vulnerable — is that this offering will "engross the attention of passersby" … that as they wander by the stove, they'll pause to listen and then pull up a chair to hear more.

An Ordinary Fishing Story

I hesitate to mention this fishing story. The details are hardly extraordinary, or even noteworthy. The episode, in fact, is quite ordinary.

Most angling adventures (when written) feature exotic settings. A mountain stream. Or the Gulf of Mexico where the trophy catches lurk. Or a Canadian chain-of-lakes reachable only by a plane, equipped with pontoons. Each of these exist seemingly far from human habitation or the commonplace; locales accessible only to the hardy, daring outdoorsman.

But this account has no such pretensions. The event occurred last summer. We were at a small pond near the entrance of Tyler Creek Recreation Area— a combination campground and golf course. We "rough it" there from time to time with our pop-up. Among the frills of the place— besides hot showers, electricity, and a park store— is this pond, stocked with bluegills, trout, and the elusive bass. For a $2-a-day fee you fish from the shore (which is a mowed lawn that surrounds the small body of water) among the scattered shade trees. There's no "getting away from it" here. Cars and motor homes go back and forth on a nearby entrance drive. Tyler Creek, itself— a shallow, rippling, and quite scenic brook— runs along one side of the pond, a narrow strip of ground separating them. Campers float down the creek on top of tubes, or enjoy strolling on the path beside it.

Close by is another attraction— a pen of farm animals that the campground proprietors called a petting zoo. Calves, sheep, goats, and pigs reside here during the warm-weather season. Here, too, located on the pathway between the pond and creek, is a rabbit hutch. Beyond all that, with the creek serving as the natural boundary, is the back nine of the golf course.

Bradley and I had fished during our previous stays, and, on this visit, we decided to do so again. The evening before we had driven into Freeport, located four miles away, and purchased a dozen night crawlers. That was more than we'd need, but the store didn't sell this bait in lesser quantities.

"I don't touch them," my young son informed the store clerk as we paid for the crawlers and other camping supplies.

"The worms are OK," the amused lady answered. "It's unhooking the fish that I dislike. How about you?"

"My dad does that," Bradley said.

"I hope we have that problem tomorrow," I offered.

At about ten o'clock in the morning— after a hearty breakfast of eggs, bacon and toast— the two of us strolled off with poles, tackle boxes, night crawlers, and a bucket.

The grass was still wet from the dew. Otherwise the setting proved pleasant— sunny, warm, and only a touch humid. We found a spot under a tree, and I began baiting the hooks. Bradley, meanwhile, made a beeline for the rabbit pen. Built on stilts, it's about three feet off the ground— kid level.

"Don't you want to cast out?" I asked him.

"No, I want to feed the bunnies," he said, pulling a handful of grass for that purpose.

So much for those well-intended father-son fishing plans. I went ahead, sans Bradley, and sent the line out into the still waters, then turned the bucket upside down and sat on it. I didn't expect much interest from the fish this late in the morning; nevertheless, having gotten used to such disinterest over the years, I was content to bask here for an hour or so.

The bluegills apparently were not done feeding. I began getting nibbles; the red-and-white bobber jerked up and down, then zig-zagged, before finally going under the surface. I set the hook, felt the ensuing pull, and started retrieving the line.

"I got one!" I called over to the rabbit observer. "You want to bring it in?" I added, thinking this might whet his angling appetite.

"Yeah, yeah!" he said as he rushed over. He turned the reel rapidly, and within seconds the gill dangled above the pond's surface. I reluctantly abandoned my seat, put water in the pail, and deposited the squirming catch.

"You want to fish now?" I asked.

"No, I want to look at the bunnies," he replied and headed back to his farm work.

We continued in this fashion. I would get one, and Bradley would bring the fish briskly into shore; I would unhook it, and he would resume his study of rabbits.

Yet, while he lacked the desire to do the necessary (and at times boring) work of waiting for a gill to bite, the young fellow did express pride in our achievement. This occurred when a father and young daughter, having visited the zoo, wandered by us and the father asked, "Having any luck?"

"Yes," my son answered on our behalf. "We've gotten a lot." At this point I'd caught five keepers. "You can look at them in our pail if you want," Bradley added.

The man did so, showing his little girl the bluegills, oohing and aahing as Bradley, standing guard, told how he'd brought them in.

Having gotten this positive feedback, he then decided (after they left) to try casting himself. But patience was not to prevail. After about five minutes he wondered when he'd be done. "I want to go swimming in the pool," he explained.

"A couple more tries," I said, deciding a dip in cool water seemed an excellent idea. We managed to land another one, giving us a half-dozen, and headed back to the camping area.

Later that afternoon the moment arrived to clean our fish. I spread out the newspapers to cover the table, proving again the versatility of journalistic enterprise. Surprisingly, my son—squeamish about worms and unhooking wigging bluegills— was gung-ho to cut up and scale the catch. Not wanting him to get hurt, I insisted on slicing off the heads and cleaning out the insides. Bradley occupied himself by using his scaling knife to poke the severed heads.

After rinsing off the fish and throwing away the layer of wet, bloody papers and the offal, we began the next cleaning step. While I held each one, Bradley used his knife to scrap off the scales, his first-ever attempt at this.

"Are they still alive?" he inquired after I had severed the heads; not sure since there remained some movement. In a follow-up question, he wondered, "Why do fish have scales?"

I managed a sufficient answer (I felt) to the 'alive' query, explaining why the fish kept twitching despite the fish being, for all purposes, dead. The question on 'scales' I found to be a more difficult matter. Hopefully, a father who can adequately deal with at least half of his kid's assorted questions is doing a fair job. Fifty percent is about my average.

Bradley's first couple of cleaning attempts on our catch had mixed results. He kept moving the blade towards the tail rather than against the grain. I finished them off for him, again demonstrating the technique. By the last two he had kind of figured out the task and only a little touching up was needed. "Will he be as eager to volunteer for this part of the fishing trip when he gets a bit older?" I asked myself.

That evening, for supper, I floured our modest mess and fried them in butter, sprinkling on a dab of salt and pepper. I'd previously asked Bradley if he wanted one or two to eat. He politely declined and instead fixed a peanut butter and jelly sandwich.

I planned to share. Still, with only six to consume, I offered just once. I saw little need to press the issue. I had baited the hook, cast the line, and caught the gills. Bradley, in turn, reeled each shoreward.

I unhooked them. He got to brag about our success to the passersby. We both cleaned them. And now I got to eat all of them.

The two of us sat at the picnic table, enjoying our respective meals and the impending twilight at Tyler Creek. The pleasant crackling of the camp fire awaited us. I decided, all-in-all (a little selfishly perhaps) that this was indeed a most suitable division of labor and reward, a fine ending to this fishing story.

Lessons in Art

My son's second-grade class at Southeastern Elementary took a field trip in late May to Michigan State University. I served as one of four adult chaperones— but the only male— with five of the youngsters assigned to my specific care. Those five included my son Bradley, Merissa, Tyler, Jennifer and Robert.

We four grown-ups, plus the teacher, Cindy Bender, seemed an adequate amount of adult firepower, enough of us to keep the fledglings under watchful eye and behaving within reasonable bounds.

Our itinerary included a brief visit to the MSU Museum of Natural History to see the replicated dinosaur skeletons— or "bones" as the kids called them— and the various other exhibits on display, with each chaperone taking his or her group on a tour as each saw fit. This stop would be followed by a guided tour of the Kresge Art Museum, a picnic lunch alongside the Red Cedar River, and then a visit to the campus's horticultural gardens. Inclement weather would have changed the latter two scheduled events, sending us instead over to the MSU Union for lunch and some board games. Fortunately, we enjoyed a balmy spring day for our journey to this bastion of higher learning.

The tour at Kresge Art Museum was the main focus of the outing. The class had watched a video earlier in the week, preparing them for the outing. This presentation apparently combined highlights of art on display at the museum which the children would see, and ground rules for proper youthful behavior. The rules, I was to learn, would be much stressed.

When I first learned that the visit to the MSU Museum of Natural History would last about half an hour, I thought it was too short a period, affording too little time to do any justice to all the place offers. "Why not just go over to the Art Museum and spend more time there?" I wondered. By the end of the afternoon I realized the wisdom of the schedule. Getting off the bus, the kids brimmed with excitement and energy. The chaperon was like a flimsy dike trying to hold back the flood waters. Or at least that's how I felt. Maybe the ladies were in better command of the situation.

Each of my five charges wanted to see something different. Once we arrived at a spot, they were eager to move on. The "bones" held their interest briefly, but then it was "What's next?" The exuberance reminded me a bit of the frenzy a youngster can get caught up in when opening Christmas or birthday presents. The actual gift being unwrapped never equals the awaiting wrapped one. They're in such a hurry that the special occasion is quickly finished, with nothing lingered over.

Lingering over stuff, I guess, is an acquired behavior. At the start I attempted a couple of times to explain what we were looking at, and two of the children (my son wasn't one of them) paused to listen. The other three wanted to push ahead, and I needed to bark "Hold up!" several times. Finally, I resorted to the voice of discipline (a sound they're apparently used to) and managed to keep my flock within eyesight and partially attentive. My game plan from then on was to keep my remarks short and to the point (a truly difficult task) and not remain still for more than a few seconds. Once we got the hang of each other's expectations— their urge to fidget and scurry versus my desire to toss them a few morsels of information and keep them within view— the final part of our tour went fine. Co-operation is, most often, best accomplished as a two-way street.

The ultimate responsibility of the chaperone, however, is not to teach, but rather to keep the children out of harm's way. After that, the goal (I feel) is to allow them some fun while keeping their instinct to become an unruly mob in check. The possibility that a kid might get lost, badly hurt, or snatched away looms large on the chaperone's mind. Mom and dad, busy at work or home, have turned this child over to the auspices of the school, and the school has now entrusted you with the duties of care and supervision. Neither parents nor school administrators expect you to be focusing intently at the fossils from the Jurassic period while the unseen boy or girl decides to climb up on the railing that protects one from the long drop down the stairs.

Hopefully, we didn't stir up too much historical dust, or ruffle too many academic feathers with our noise and quick pace. If possible, maybe we would have been well-advised to haul the class over to Spartan Stadium before starting our tour, run them up and down the field a few times and then wander, quiet, slow, and tired past the exhibits.

Burning off part of this excess of youthful fuel proved a wise prelude before we headed over to the more orderly sanctum of the art world. As it turned out, even then a good deal of energy still managed to flow out of the channels that the art docents have constructed. I shudder to think what we would have faced if this more sedate and confined domain had been our initial stop of the morning.

At the Kresge Museum, the 21 students were split into three groups with two docents guiding each one. I now had two extra children to oversee, although I soon felt more like the eighth kid rather than one of the authority figures.

We began— all three groups— by sitting cross-legged on the floor, scattered in a semi-circle around the head docent, a gray-haired lady who sat on a bench as she made her presentation. I found a spot to the side and, being an older fellow, decided to lean up against the wall. One of the other docents came over and gently told me that "the children are asked not to touch the walls, so perhaps you'd better not." Thus began my lesson on art appreciation and proscribed behavior.

This lesson was soon reinforced. The head docent, noting that the children had seen the video, added: "We have some rules here. What are they?" The kids raised their hands and were individually called by name, the lady checking their name tags. "No yelling and no running" were offered. A couple other answers were given. Then one of the students said, "No touching."

"No touching," the docent repeated the phrase. "That's probably the most important rule." I hadn't seen the video so I had an excuse for being the first one to violate this prohibition.

The lady then commenced with her talk, a very interesting and instructive one, by introducing us to "the line" and connotations it can give or suggest. During her discourse, the information was not conveyed by lecture. Rather she asked the boys and girls "what" they saw or thought, letting them offer their answers or, more often, possibilities.

The horizontal line, the kids agreed, suggests rest or repose. The vertical line implies a feeling of motion, as does the diagonal line. The wavy line appears more tranquil and soothing than the harsh, jagged line. The way an artist use lines, the lady said, helps them communicate these connotations. She pointed out that lines can be drawn as shapes. There are the recognizable ones like circles, squares, and triangles, and those that are unique, created by individual imagination. The use of lines also makes patterns. She held up a note card with a series of vertical and horizontal lines intersecting to form small squares and, thus, a mesh pattern.

Color, she added, also conveys an impression. Some colors look loud and brash, and others seem calmer and more subtle.

We then got up, split into our groups of seven, and made our respective tours of different art. The head docent led my small band, and proved to be a rules-oriented person. While her lessons about art were instructive and seemed well-geared for these young elementary students, they were liberally sprinkled with mild cautions. She was as mindful, I suppose, of being a chaperone of the art as well as being a teacher. The kids weren't overtly breaking any rules, other than a minor inadvertent infraction of the sort I committed. They were "just kids" and so, I guess, looked and acted like they might do so— and maybe would have without the reminders.

Our tour began with two antique automobiles, one of them featuring a wooden body. The cars were surrounded by a protective rope and the opening comment was "not to touch the rope." The docent asked the kids what differences they saw between these cars and the modern ones they rode in. Several children raised their hands, and she called on them. No glass windows, different roofs, and the one car having a wooden body were offered as answers. The guide pointed out that the seating wouldn't allow more than two or three people to ride, and there was little trunk space. "You couldn't take many people or go on long trips, could you?" she noted.

We moved over to an enclosed glass display case with various automobile hood ornaments; all of them ornate in appearance and most from bygone years. Again the children were warned not to touch the glass and "to stand back." A brief explanation about the ornaments was given, some of their specific histories, and then the lady took us over to an unusual sculpture.

Small colored circles had been placed on the floor around the work. Our hostess told the kids to find a circle and stand on it. Two of the youngsters started to quarrel, each of them wanting to occupy the same spot. The teacher, Mrs. Bender, was fortunately nearby and quickly settled the dispute, saving me from having to intervene. But then she got scolded soon after for taking a picture of the scene, and using the flash. We learned that a flashing camera was another "no, no" at the art museum. I felt better about my indiscretion with the wall, no longer being the lone adult offender.

The sculpture had a metal pyramid base. Balanced horizontally on its apex was a narrow metal rod. Attached to one end of the rod was a rendition of the sun, while at the opposite end were offshoots that, at their tips, had small circular pieces. The kids offered and the docent agreed that these circular objects represented planets and stars. The docent then blew gently on the sun, and the horizontal section began to revolve, demonstrating how well-balanced the artist had made this replica of the heavens and why the circles on the floor had been placed at that precise distance from the sculpture.

We next looked at a painting. This consisted of a large canvas with wide vertical strokes of varying colors spaced out in intervals across the light background. The painting consisted of a black stroke and the rest a combination of pairs; two light purples, two dark purples, two light blues, two dark blues, and so on. The pairs, though, were not side by side, but mixed together.

Our docent explained that the canvas had been tilted when the artist applied the strokes of paint, starting at the top and brushing and letting it run downward. You could see moisture stains, now dried, along the edges of several of the strokes. She talked a little about the use of color and asked if the painting showed movement?

The kids replied "No." An incorrect answer, I thought. However, she let their judgment stand uncontested. Perhaps that's a rule for art guides: do not challenge the interpretation of the observer, novices though most of us are. While I'm not inclined to criticize or be dismissive of art I don't understand, I couldn't grasp the point of this painting. Its significance escaped me. "What made it worth having in a museum?" I wondered. Fortunately, she didn't ask for my interpretation. The best response I might have given is that the color is both pattern and random.

Our group fared better when questioned on a dimensional piece, answering that the painting is a two-dimensional piece of art while the sculpture is three-dimensional.

Next we saw a gallery of photographs. The common theme of this display was the automobile, specifically its use by people and its impact on life. I'm assuming that the museum happened to be spotlighting the automobile at the time of our visit.

"Photographers often try to tell us something with their pictures," the lady said.

The first photo we saw was a black and white photo of several Cadillac cars sticking vertically out of the sand, all of them in a neat row. Its title was 'Cadillac Cemetery.'

The next one, more evident in its meaning, showed an old discarded car in the foreground, while in the background were the wooden buildings— looking equally dilapidated— of a coal mining town. "This shows a place without much money, doesn't it?" the docent asked the children.

"Or without hope of opportunity," I thought.

A third photo— most arresting of all— had been taken during the 1930s Depression. The guide explained that the mother and two children shown sitting in their car, with the passenger door open, were living in it. Food cans and blankets could be seen in the back seat. The mother and her kids had dirty faces, and looked weary and forlorn. "You wouldn't want to live in your car, would you?" the guide asked.

For once, the young second graders did not push towards the art, nor need to be reminded to “stand back.” Maybe they reflexively, like many of us, wished to keep such reality, past or present, at arm’s length. This art possessed power. Even as you sought to pull away, the picture draws you into the plight of the mother and her small children.

Our tour continued with a grated steel door. Here our opening lessons about ‘the line’ and shapes and patterns were put to use. The students were asked which of the bars were horizontal, vertical, and diagonal. The diagonal ones had been used to form a series of small X’s, with small spheres attached to each end of the X. The lines, of course, formed certain patterns, and this was pointed out by our guide.

From there, we went to what, our docent explained, had once been part of a floor dating back to the Roman Empire. The remnant consisted of miniature square tiles. These tiles, in turn, had a mosaic painted on them that depicted the Greek myth of Achilles’ mother— the goddess Thetis married to the mortal Peleus— who sought to make her son immortal by dipping him, when he was a baby, into the River Styx. She held him by his heel while doing so, and, as a consequence, this was the only part of his body not submerged into the Stygian water. Achilles, as both a man and a warrior in the Trojan War, was invulnerable to any fatal wounds except for that part of his foot. As any student of Greek mythology would know, and as our second graders were informed, Achilles was subsequently killed by an arrow shot into that unprotected heel by Paris.

The museum also featured a special exhibit of posters for the Olympic Games – 1896 to present. When we reached this part of the tour, another lady took over the narration. She appeared newer to this guiding business and bubbled with enthusiasm. Afterwards she told me that she “really enjoyed my kids” and was “sorry we didn’t have more time.” The kids responded to her personality and liked the subject matter, so they tended to crowd around each of the posters we viewed. This prompted the head docent, and by now yours truly, to request that they stand back, and remind them not to touch.

In fairness to our hostess (the head docent), while she stressed the rules, she also took a shine to one of the boys who’d stumbled over a couple answers early on, and started to retreat from the experience. She made an extra effort to get him back into the flow, and it paid off. By the end of our poster presentation he’d become an eager contributor.

First off, we learned that the five Olympic rings (symbolizing the five continents that send athletes to the games) were located somewhere in every poster. But, it was noted, they are not always noticeable. The kids got excited about finding the rings each time we went on to a new poster. The Olympics include both summer and winter games, so we began with the recent ones held in Atlanta, Georgia and in Norway, and made it as far back as the 1968 summer games before our allotted time ran out.

The docent explained what abstract art is, and how it attempts to create an image or impression of real objects rather than being a more realistic or photographic rendition. She also noted that posters, like these for the Olympics, serve as an advertising medium. Since most of these posters utilized abstract art, the kids were asked what the different images reminded them of, or what the particular poster was depicting.

One jagged pattern, with blue above and white below, drawn on the bottom half of a Winter Olympics' poster, bewildered me for a moment until I saw that the white symbolized steep snow-covered mountains with the blue representing the sky. The top half of another poster, definitely an abstract piece of art, had a picture of the feet and lower legs of modern track athletes, showing them wearing their shoes, while the bottom half was the familiar drawing of the legs of the ancient Greek Olympians. The youngsters, being young, aren't yet familiar with the latter drawing, so the docent quickly explained how the original games began over 2,700 years ago in ancient Greece (and lasted over 11 centuries) and that the athletes competed in their bare feet. Olympians, in modern times, use footwear. The poster, by showing this juxtaposition, gave a sense of those long ago roots of this now international extravaganza.

The guide neglected to mention that those ancient Greeks (all males) were bare all over, not just their feet. They competed in their running, wrestling and throwing events without any hindrance of clothes. I'm sure she was well acquainted with this fact, but was mindful that young elementary-aged children would turn into a giggling gaggle, and the rest of the lesson would be lost on them as they laughed at the thought of bare-naked people running around.

As we were looking at the poster of the 1968 games which had been held in Mexico City, the bell rang, signaling the end to this part of the tour. The artist of this poster had drawn what seemed like jagged circles. To me they looked fiery, and I envisioned the hot sun and the Aztec Empire when I gazed at them. My son, unaware of the Aztecs, told the lady they resembled tornadoes. He's been fascinated with tornadoes for two-to-three years now, and had drawn them frequently during his previous (first grade) year in school. He is a big fan of the twister in *The Wizard of Oz.* Someone else claimed the jagged circles resembled fireworks or explosions. The unspoken lesson here was that our background, experiences, interests, knowledge, and age can, and usually do determine what we see or feel about a given piece of art. We hold different views because we possess differing outlooks. While we share much in common, we are blessed as well with individual distinctiveness.

At this point our group of seven was reunited with the other two student groups. The kids received paper, crayons, and pencils and were then given a short period of time to draw their own Olympic posters. The only requirement was that the five connected rings—three on top and two below— be included somewhere.

The tour ended on a high note: many of them actually. We gathered around a sculpture. Here we saw reed-like stems emerge upward from a solid, square base. Atop each stem (or reed) was a cylinder-shaped piece, resembling a patch of cattails. A young lady, wearing white gloves, bunched the cylinders together and then released them.

The resulting sounds went from loud to soft as the tops struck each other and drew apart. Added to the sound was the vibration moving down the stem and making an echo.

"If this was outside, how would the sounds be caused?" the children were asked.

"The wind?" several immediately replied.

"What does the sound remind you of?" was another question.

"Bells," one student said.

"Wind chimes" was my silent answer. The museum piece sounded similar to those chimes that once hung outside our bedroom window, adding a bit of music whenever a breeze stirred; heard mainly at night as we drifted off to sleep. Having had those melodious sounds recalled to me, I might buy another set, and again enjoy this musical repose.

We then left for our lunch. We sat on the mowed lawn, near the museum and beside the slow-moving waters of the Red Cedar. The blooming magnolia trees and other flowering bushes added their beauty to the scenery. Nature and Man, I thought, have combined forces to create landscape art),

* * *

As we made our tour of Kresge Art Museum, I found myself as conscious of obeying the rules (the "Do Not Touches") and of making sure the kids didn't get in trouble with the docent as I was of the lessons in art appreciation. Certainly, had I been alone or on a family outing with my wife and son, the rules might not have been repeated so often; thus they would have been less noticeable.

This experience with the youngsters, however, offered an interesting consideration. Artists, by reputation, including the ones I've known, tend to be bohemians, and often rebels. Pushers against the status quo. Challengers of the accepted norms. Benders of the straight line. Yet, these academic guardians of their artistic output seem to have erected a format that felt rigid. A sense of constriction existed which seems contrary to the intent many artists have concerning accessibility to their work.

Having said that, I realize that rules of behavior and conduct are necessary. You can't have a couple dozen children ramming around the museum, doing as they like. Many of the art pieces are fragile, irreplaceable, or valuable. Additionally, this activity would be unfair to others in attendance. And little can be learned without listening, and behaving in a quiet manner. This tour wasn't, after all, the playground, but an extension of the classroom.

While the kids were busy drawing their posters, I approached the ladies who had conducted the tour and told them that I'd learned one thing.

"What's that?" one of them asked.

"That kids this age have an almost irresistible urge to touch," I said.

The docents laughed. "They do, don't they?" another agreed.

I added (with irony intended, but not any malice) that "Part of the so-called civilizing process is to get them not to."

The sensation of touch, along with sight, sound, smell, and taste help us comprehend the world around us. The baby learns about the nature of an object, and therefore life, by putting it in his or her mouth. The youngster touches to better understand, by feel, just what this object is all about.

We find through trial and error— as well as reprimand— that not everything should, or can be tasted or touched. And as we grow older, we trust the eye, ear, nose, or a combination of these, along with a more developed capacity of reasoning— of deduction and induction — to figure out the nature and essence of an object. Still, I doubt if any of us ever completely outgrow this desire to reach out, and to run our fingers across a surface new to us, to determine if the sensation is equal to what the other senses are conjecturing. The touch usually surpasses such speculation. Imagination can never replace "the real thing."

But human touch, singly and accumulatively, can be destructive. The elements of Nature— heat, cold, moisture, and wind— given enough time, will eventually threaten many of our artistic as well as other creations. Human presence and admiration often speed the deteriorative process. From smog to the friction of thousands of footsteps upon the cathedral stairs, to the residue from an oily fingerprint, each of these, added to many other acts and activities, can directly or indirectly cause damage. In fact, sometimes our admiration of the arts is as threatening, or more so, as is neglect, indifference, or even hostility. The lone vandal might inflict more immediate scars. But a few thousand touches by an appreciative public can eventually cause a more destructive result.

In attempting to achieve a proper balance between protection and accessibility, perhaps it's important to ask the questions: What constitutes art? and What is the purpose, intent, or worth of art?

Art can be esthetic or utilitarian, but often are a mix of the two. The Olympic posters we saw were works of creativity, yet were informative. They both pleased the senses *and* promoted the event. The grated steel door was ornate— an elaborately designed and well-crafted piece of expressive metal work and welding— and still served the function of a door.

Certainly, not all efforts need to have a useful or easily-understood application to qualify as admired works of art. That said, one of the lessons these exhibits at Kresge demonstrated is that art is not just found in museums, existing apart from our daily routines and more well-known surroundings. Quite the contrary. The styling of your chair, the dining room buffet, the photograph in the magazine, the novel on the bed stand, the architecture of a church or courthouse, the engraving on a dollar bill, along with the painting hung above the fireplace fall under the heading of art. Some art may be more decorative, without practical application. Other works may be so ordinary and familiar that we miss the touch of the artist at work.

Art, though, goes beyond utility and esthetics. It can cause us to view ourselves, or the life around us, from different perspectives. The work might challenge our preconceptions or smug attitudes; it may even awaken our lazy senses. Artists often explore new intellectual or emotional territory. As mentioned, they can also illuminate what's right before us, but which we'd heretofore overlooked, ignored, dismissed, or viewed as insignificant. Art can be an attempt to give our lives, and all life, added meaning by providing better explanations through the use of image and expression. The outcome can be jolting in its impact, or simply fun. It can enrich us and reward our curiosity and imagination. But it can, likewise, cause trouble, or even prompt anger, since not all art is inherently ethical and benevolent and because both the artist and patron hold subjective, sometimes partisan outlooks.

If the work does impact you, then it can become a seed that grows with continued nourishment into a fruit. Or, if it's slightly nagging or bothersome, a grain of sand that over time and with further contemplation, forms into a personal pearl.

Not all art is *advent guard*, or seeks to upset the apple cart. Not all artistic efforts should. There are works that seek to celebrate the status quo, reinforce the accepted, and maintain the straight line. And, every now and then, art that's whimsical or light-and-frothy is just fine.

So, should art (at least those works judged as unique and valuable) be exposed to the grit and grim of the here-and-now, or be kept at arm's length from our curious and admiring touch? Is the greater worth and potential found in making it more remote—to be left for future judgment? Yet, if we treat art as too special for the present, make it inaccessible or inadvertently make people (young and old) feel alien to it, then art can lose its connection to the people it was supposedly created to reach. We risk turning off or scaring away people by making art seem too high-toned. The creative work, thus, loses is chance to impact and to do its own 'touching.'

On the other hand, if we treat art as only being valuable for its immediate benefits, if its main purpose is to serve the here-and-now, then we might fail to give these works a chance to become legacies and artifacts of our time; to be seen as masterpieces by the future.

When a child reaches out "to feel" the art, is our allegiance to that moment of wonder; or to the rule that protects the piece? Which is the greater loss? Is it the child who turns away when scolded or the object that sustains the ever-so slight wreckage?

I don't know. When I looked at the seven kids I was chaperoning, I could see that a couple of them were bored with the whole experience, and I knew that this kind of creativity would probably never consciously be an important part of their future routines. Others seemed interested and were teetering on the brink. As for providing this educational adventure to them regardless of the future outcome, I applaud the teacher (Cindy Bender), the docents, and Kresge.

Maybe the answer is that we need certain areas in the art museums where kids (and adults) can touch. But then, no doubt, we'll debate whether the "touched" art is as valuable or important as the "protected" stuff. I quite agree that it's difficult to appreciate and understand anything when chaos prevails, and whim goes unchecked. A measure of restraint and orderliness are often necessary. "Yes," there should be a responsibility to preserve art as best possible so that others— now and in the future— can share it. Still, I can't quite accept the *line* "as is." I need to bend it with another question. As I watch those kids, my son included, lean forward, so eager to reach out, and as I heard the repeated cautions, I wondered: "If a creative work compels within you an urge to touch it, and there is a rule that constrains and forbids you from doing so, then is this work really art… or just a reflection?"

Echoes from Past Novembers

Part 1

Math was the focus of my attention at that moment. I sat in Riby Holmes' class, puzzling (as usual) over a problem— "problem" being an accurate description for a mathematical question— when our principal announced over the P.A. system that President Kennedy had been shot. Shortly afterwards we learned, again over the P.A., that he had died.

With me in that room were about a quarter of that year's Fowlerville seventh grade enrollment. We attended classes in the building (at what was then the high school) which housed the seventh-thru-twelfth grades. The building, now over forty years old, currently serves as the middle school. Soon, with completion of a new junior high, it will serve fifth and sixth graders. The population around here has grown considerably since JFK reigned on the Potomac.

The seventh and eighth grades were on half-day sessions that fall; there were too many of us (along with the high school students) to squeeze into the available space. Work, though was nearly finished on a small addition to the north corridor that would allow the junior high to resume a full-day schedule. This wouldn't occur, however, until the start of the second semester in mid-January.

So, during those first 18 weeks of the 1963-64 school year the eighth graders arrived in the morning with the high schoolers and left at mid day. Then we (seventh graders) showed up, took our four classes— math, science, social studies, and English— and departed at day's end with our upper classmates.

It was a great schedule. I realized how "great it was" after the novelty of the full day— with the addition of home room, band, gym, and study hall— had worn off. My mornings included a few farm chores, whatever homework was required, and then a nice chunk of time left for leisurely activities. There were no siblings (my younger sister and brother) to contend with; they being on full days. My mother would feed me a nice lunch. I remember specifically enjoying her recently-canned peaches. At age 12, this abbreviated school day was just the ticket.

Late in the morning I'd climb aboard a nearly empty bus. The passengers consisted of three or four fellow seventh graders and a like number of afternoon kindergartners. We had a tranquil jaunt about the neighborhood, and then rode into town. That scenario was completely opposite from the rigors and noise of the packed bus later in the day. I didn't get hassled too often by the older lads— no more than any other younger target (and much less than a couple of unfortunate victims)— still, it happened enough to make me wary, and prefer the earlier ride.

Many events were canceled or postponed in the wake of the Kennedy assassination. From the confused hours after the murder until the playing of *Taps* at Arlington Cemetery and the lighting of the eternal flame, most of us, young and old, kept vigil as much as possible in front of the TV. When the funeral ended, the citizenry, mirroring a stunned and grieving family, got up and slowly resumed their normal everyday activities. Yet, while we, as a nation, resumed those familiar patterns, we were no longer quite the same.

I'm unable to recall or even guess what might have prompted it, but John Kennedy and politics had captured my youthful fancy in the summer of 1960 when I turned nine. I had declared myself a Kennedy partisan after the Democratic Convention, and his nomination. That put me in the minority hereabouts. As far as I know, most of my relatives and most of Fowlerville preferred Richard Nixon and the Republicans. I had also fervently embraced the Detroit Tigers and baseball earlier that year, so I was apparently inclined at this impressionable stage of life towards making ardent attachments.

I joined only a handful of kids in the gym of our elementary school during noon-hour recess to watch the Kennedy inauguration. The rest, either being disappointed Nixon supporters, or more likely unimpressed by the occasion, chose to romp outside in the snow. In retrospect, tossing snowballs and climbing the monkey bars was, and still is, probably a wiser choice for youngsters than meddling in politics.

Among the events postponed by the assassination was the Michigan State-Illinois college football game. Each autumn our 4-H club from Conway Township, being part of MSU's Cooperative Extension Service and no doubt getting a discounted price for tickets as a result of this affiliation, attended a Spartan game. The contest that year had championship implications and was delayed until six days later. That afternoon we watched Illinois defeat our home team by a 13-0 score and qualify for a trip to the Rose Bowl. One of the names the announcer constantly repeated, due to his ferocious defensive work, was Illinois linebacker Dick Butkus. He also played center for their offense. While my awareness of sports had been expanding, this game was the first time I'd heard of Butkus. I normally paid attention, like many other fans, to the quarterbacks, runners, and ends. Hard-hitting linebackers, with Butkus destined to become among the best in college and the NFL, soon got included.

So, along with daydreaming of hitting .300 and scoring numerous touchdowns, I began imagining myself (despite being a lightweight in those earlier years) as one of these renowned defensive players. Like many of my youthful notions, ensuing reality held a more mundane outcome. As far as athletic talents and skills, I proved to be rather average. No "glory days" were to await me on the playing fields.

The passion for politics also eventually cooled from my initial boyhood ardor, although the flames took longer to ebb. Still, the interest has never quite disappeared; the embers from that initial enthusiasm still glow. For awhile at the tail end of my high school years, and when I first started college, I had seen this arena as a possible career; my plan being to combine it with my desire to write. But, for a variety of reasons and due to a number of circumstances, I followed a different path. Instead of jumping into the political fray, I've ended up operating on the outskirts as reporter… more a spectator than a partisan. I now observe politics, along with sports and all the rest— serious and less so—that takes place. And, every so often when the spirit moves me, I ponder (as I'm best able) the possible meaning of it all… overarching, underlying, or beyond my comprehension.

Our perception and how we experience events— whether personal, historical, or a combination of each— can create odd bedfellows. The Kennedy assassination, Riby Holmes and his math class, home-canned peaches, and Dick Butkus, for better or worse, rest together in my (sometimes rambling) mind.

Part 2

On a November evening in 1967 my father died of heart failure. He was 38 and had been in and out of the hospital during the preceding months. His prognosis had not been encouraging; even so, we did not think this condition put him in immediate danger.

The death of a loved one obviously causes interruptions and disruptions in the routines of family and friends. As it should. Still, the flywheel of habit, the necessities and responsibilities of life and living, move us onward.

For me, at age 16 and the eldest child, the cows needed milking and the chores needed doing. Other than the afternoon of the funeral when our neighbor, Bill Schoonover, did both, I attended to those duties. Another neighbor, Loris McCallum, also assisted us. He came over for three or four milkings during those couple of confusing days after my dad's sudden death, offering to do whatever he could.

After each milking I thanked him. Loris muttered that he hadn't done much. I was young, knew what came next, and moved quickly. He was about 65 then and, although he had been a dairy farmer, he was unfamiliar with our barn and our sequence of tasks. So, in a literal sense he was probably correct. But having him there, talking with him every so often, helped. His presence, his sadness, and the silent yet evident desire to console were what mattered most.

His own son and only child, Jim, had died of a heart attack the year before. Jim was even younger than my father, about 27. Dad had gone over and helped milk their cattle as Loris and Margaret struggled with their unexpected loss, continuing this help until the funeral and burial were over. While my father assisted them at their place, I handled our small herd, alone, which was something I could do by then when necessary.

I understood that Loris, besides wishing to offer his sympathy, had come to our barn to return the kindness shown to him and his wife by my father. He did so with that gesture, as well as many others over the ensuing months. I realize now, and maybe I did even back then, that as he sat on a stool, watching me as I worked, that the death of my father, a young neighbor and fellow farmer, had probably re-opened the still raw wounds of grief for his son. The two had occurred close enough together to give them an emotional link.

Loris and Margaret were friends of both my grandparents and my folks. I grew up in regular contact with them and Jim. The McCallums owned a small farm a little over a mile away, and, along with milking a few cows, operated a livestock hauling business. On many a Monday Loris showed up at our place (or at my grandparents) to take the bull calves or an old cow to the Howell Sale. He also transported our 4-H heifers and cows to and from the fair each July.

In addition, my grandfather, father, and Uncle Rollie would hire him to bale their straw and second cutting of hay. He or Jim would drive over with their tractor and baler along with two wagons, and we'd go to work. Apparently somewhere along the line, my elders had decided it was more expedient to contract for this service than to buy and maintain the necessary equipment. The bulk of our dry hay was chopped and then blown into the barn lofts— a dirtier business on a windy or hot-and-humid day, but much less labor intensive than baling.

Besides those numerous contacts, my mother would invite Margaret and Loris over for Sunday dinner. Other times they'd come over to watch a special event, like the Rose Bowl Parade, on our new color TV; a color set still being a novelty in those mid-1960s' days.

The summer after Dad died we were ready to sell the cows and machinery. The McCullums, who had already sold their milking cattle after losing Jim, had reached the same decision; to leave farming. A combined auction was held at their place.

We subsequently re-located to a new home my mother had had built in a subdivision north of town. However, my farming days were not yet over. With our cows gone, I began helping my grandfather with the evening milking, as well as with the assorted chores and field work. This would remain my after-school, weekend, and summer job until I moved to a college dormitory. I still helped on occasion during the next few years. Finally, the day arrived (a day of which I have no recollection) when I milked my last cow at my grandparents' farm, and performed my final chore.

Loris kept the livestock truck, and our paths still crossed after the auction, only less often until our lives no longer intersected. They certainly could have. But young men in a hurry do not always realize the eventual regrets that will come by such choice, in this case of omission.

Death, unexpected and sudden, had intruded into our respective and shared worlds. A son lost; a father gone. Each of us was the same, yet no longer quite the same. Then the trajectories of our daily routines, once moving in similar directions, and in close proximity, gradually veered away from each other, and they continued doing so until one day Loris, too, died. Then only one trajectory remained. And memory.

Part 3

During my brief adventure in San Francisco in the autumn of '72, I struggled over a piece of writing I'd entitled *A Ballad of the '60s*. Of course I struggled with nearly everything I attempted to write in my younger days. I still do for that matter.

Borrowing from the format used in Hemingway's *In Our Time* and John Dos Possos's *USA Trilogy*, I sought to intermingle vignettes of famous people, news headlines, and fictional short stories— a mix of historical and personal episodes that would span the decade during which I had only recently grown up in and come of age. It would be a combination that (I thought) would enlighten and illuminate. To accomplish part of the necessary research, I would often walk over to the public library, a massive concrete structure located on one end of the public square across from the city Hall. I'd sit at a table, look up the assorted information in available reference textbooks, and take notes. It also meant sitting at the card table in my room, with paper and pen, and reliving (via the scribbled sentences) highlights of my past; opening up old wounds in some cases.

I learned, beginning at that table, and eventually during the following years, that I possessed little aptitude for imagined narratives or invented situations; and little appetite for stories that were a thinly disguised version of my own life and would, by necessity, include the lives of those near and dear. Lacking a natural skill to make-up stories, characters, and dialogue, and not wishing to substitute this deficiency with a tell-all autobiography, I was (you could say) in a fix.

Fiction proved a frustration: a maze of dead ends. I'd get 'the bug' every so often, go at it, and then, feeling the output was flat and dull, give up; a hot pursuit that always ended with disappointment and a growing resignation. I'd sing, but my voice was off-key. Finally, a few years ago, about the time I was turning 40, I abandoned this path and instead embraced the essay and the journalistic profile.

Ah... if I'd only taken this career route sooner. Yet I actually did. I just didn't do so with planned intent and purpose and, thus, the overall effort seemed unfulfilling. I sort of drifted along, thinking I should be going somewhere else (i.e. fiction), feeling discontented with my obvious lack of progress, when I was pursuing pretty much what I needed to pursue... namely this.

That observation is offered not as a lament, but rather as an advisory caution. We're encouraged to reach far, and should. *The try* is important. Still, on occasion, we need to take stock and determine what's within our grasp, and obtainable; have a goal or an objective that we're actually capable of achieving, not one that turns into pointless obsession, or becomes a futile endeavor.

A quarter of a century ago the brass ring I sought to grab, *the try* I wished to make, was the idea of being a short-story writer. I had turned 21 that summer of '72 and felt, as an aspiring literary artist, I should remove myself from the confines of familiar surroundings and instead experience the social and cultural sensations of a cosmopolitan crossroads. The crossroads I had in mind was San Francisco— the exotic *city by the sea* romanticized in song and literature. More significantly, the city was considered a counter-culture Mecca; a safe haven where birds-of-a-feather could flock. The move was more palatable because I had friends already residing there. Fred, Laura, and Laura's three kids— Shawn, Todd, and Eric— had made the move the year before. Fred and Laura, in the letters we exchanged, urged me to come out, adding that a room was available in the building where they stayed.

Residing in San Francisco, I theorized, would serve as nourishment for my still-budding abilities and understandings. The scrawny country wildflower, transplanted into this hot house of human vegetation, might flourish and one day bloom into a substantial plant. A lofty premise. Full of youthful hubris as well as yearning. Perhaps, with more time and more determination— if I'd stuck it out— part of this scenario might have happened.

It doesn't matter. I felt then, and still do, that I'd gotten out of my element. To borrow some more from the metaphor, as a plant, this was the wrong weather, wrong soil, wrong sunlight, and wrong wind. We are what we are. I belonged where I'd come from, not here.

With little money and no saleable skills, I didn't last long on the California scene. And the place wasn't all it was cracked up to be— or, more likely, how I'd imagined it was supposed to be. Scenic, exotic, and culturally diverse? Yes. Also, tolerant of and a safe haven for the mavericks, which made the city a drawing card in those days of tense and often volatile passions caused by disagreements over the Vietnam War, civil rights, alternative lifestyles, music, politics, and social directions.

Perhaps my own circumstances altered the actual view, but the South-of-Market District where I stayed appeared more gray than pastel; not down-trodden, just a bit down-in-the-heel. A tourist might have found the area quaint. For many of the residents, however, there existed the continuous need of making sparse ends meet. As a result, the place had a few rough edges.

Additionally, some of the newcomers who had sought a tolerant safe haven were not always obliging in return. They, too, held their share of arbitrary, exclusionary and self-serving attitudes; vices they accused "the establishment" of fostering. Behind their banner of individuality and free expression lurked that same old social impulse to impose group conformity. As someone who grew up amid farmers who belonged to voluntary co-operatives, I prefer that model of social interaction and structure.

Starting with the first night, I felt a sense of having lost my bearings. I felt alone and adrift, even though I never minded being alone now and then back in Michigan. Instead of taking comfort from all of the people around me, the vast crowd only made me feel insignificant. And, thrown into this mental mix came the emerging realization— now that I was in this crossroads— that I wasn't as much the maverick I pictured myself to be.

Fred, Laura, and the kids offset some of this loneliness. They kept me company, invited me over for meals, took me on their outings, and shared what they could. Several others who lived in the building where we stayed also offered their friendship. Despite their good efforts, they couldn't offset my feeling of having made a wrong move. More and more I felt unhappy. While assisting me, my friends weren't in a position to be nursemaids, nor should they have needed to be. Twenty-one-year-old men are expected to pull their own weight. I wanted to. I just couldn't find much weight to pull.

Had I landed a paying job, I might have changed my outlook. But I didn't have much to offer the employers out there. I tried the gas stations, hotels, and restaurants for a job, without any success. 'The City', as the folks of San Francisco liked to refer to their town, overflowed with young men and women of my age; a goodly sum of them (like me) coming from other locales. It was another of those bulges of The Baby Boomer generation; too many of us trying to fill the too few available slots.

A number of my contemporaries earned their keep by panhandling, going up to pedestrians and asking for a quarter or two. These solicitors, and the piles of dog manure, were two things you quickly learned to keep an eye out for when walking and attempt to avoid as best you could.

I'd read a lot of books and heard a lot of classroom lectures during my school career. No one appeared ready to pay me to read, though. Also, there weren't any milk herds in 'The City', at least none that I was aware of, so I couldn't fall back on that acquired skill from my farm-boy days. If I could have worked cement with a trowel or welded iron, I might have been hired on the spot. Market Street, a couple blocks from where I resided, was being torn up and re-done.

Still, I've learned (since) that San Francisco is a strong trade union town, meaning that even with such abilities, quick employment might not have occurred. These opportunities, there as elsewhere, come about as much from "who you know" as "what you know." The following spring, back in Michigan, I landed a job in construction because of "who I knew."

Of course the fond dream was to avoid such labor and make my wages with the written word. I eventually succeeded in doing that through the avenue of journalism. However, newspapering (at that point in time) hadn't yet become a consideration. A few more years would come and go before I pursued this career path.

So, as those autumn days passed by back in '72, I began facing these tough facts: I didn't write well, what I did write wasn't going to make any money in the immediate future, and, in the meanwhile, I lacked any occupational know-how that might gain me employment in 'The City." Finally, there were too many of us bookworms, fresh from school, competing for a limited quantity of unskilled jobs.

Additionally, I realized the stories I was writing or attempting to write— mostly fragments— concerned my world back home, not this new place. My muse, I started to comprehend, came from the country; from plowed fields, lulling cattle, jagged horizons of greenery, pheasants flushing from the meadow, meandering rivers, and four pronounced seasons. I came to feel also that any windmills I might tilt against, any wrongs I might attempt to rectify, any ills I might seek to cure, any efforts to improve our common lot— feeble though they might ultimately be— would better be done in Michigan; in those familiar surroundings of nature and nurture.

The rural, small-town landscape and culture provides, for me, the proper balance between reflection and action; the assorted available activities (be it a hike in the woods, fishing, or sitting around a campfire) help offset the solitary confinement of writing. During my residence in San Francisco, short though it turned out to be, I discovered that having only writing and reading to occupy much of my waking hours, accompanied by a sense of limitation— both financially and with my overall prospects—made me too self-absorbed, too melancholy and introspective, even a bit morbid. Since I'm still apt to be guilty of any of those traits, I've learned that diversion is the best remedy.

I did end up walking a lot, and managed to cover a fair amount of geography during my daily treks in the afternoon. Sometimes I'd stop at a corner saloon and tip a couple while visiting with the barmaid, a red-haired lady in her early 40s named Marsha who took to being my mother hen. She'd make sure I had some of the snacks the bar offered to its customers late in the afternoon, or she'd slip me a free draft. I assume Marsha had figured out I operated on a tight budget. Mostly, she offered a cheery counterpoint to my melancholy mood. The walks and the visits, while helping to fill the empty hours, did not address my tentative situation. Thus the mood persisted and deepened.

I kept a notebook during my stay in San Francisco. The entries were an odd assortment. They included my written attempts, song lyrics, fragments of poems by Dylan Thomas and T.S. Eliot, and several excerpts from the books I'd read.

Wandering through an art and music festival, held near the library one Saturday soon after I arrived in town, I later penned:

At the grassy square/ a festival of creativity & fun/ where art is... observe the sad-eyed clown perform/ expressions of an affluent society/ pantomime of imagination/ no visions of tomorrow/ only portraits of despair

A Ballad of the '60s— those sketches of personal and larger history— came out equally doleful and dark.

"Television was the major influence of the decade," I wrote. "Described as a 'vast wasteland', it had, however, the advantage of immediacy; a voyeur at assassinations, repression, funerals, war, revolution, demonstrations, starvation, deceptions, pathos, and confrontations."

From my own past, remembering the death of my father (and its aftermath), I started a short story:

"The funeral parlor, decorated in autumn browns, gives impression of somber presence. A gray coffin, counterbalanced by trimmings of ornate brass, lined in cushioned white fabric, sits to the far end. On either side and behind, a floral display— gladioluses, chrysanthemums, and carnations blooming in summer opulence— has been arranged as careful backdrop, giving subtle contrast to death's ritual festivity."

For the vignette on John Kennedy's death, an obviously landmark event during the 1960s, I wrote not about my more accurate recollection of being in Riby Holmes' math class, but this series of fragments.

CBS afternoon/ "we interrupt this program"/ "President Kennedy assassinated!"/ blood-splattered mourning widow/ black-veiled praying mother/ tear-stained paradox nation/ Lee Harvey Oswald accused/ paint this picture crayon evening blue/ muffled cadence of the funeral procession/ ashen orb framed in cirrus gray streaks/ TV melodrama: saga of an assassin/ nightclub owner rushes in on cue

I have no memory of what I meant by "crayon evening blue", other than maybe it looked creative. Otherwise, the images hold up. I later tried to do a story of a fellow sitting in the Haystack Tavern in Fowlerville, watching this unfolding sequence on television.

Neither approach quite "hit the mark". Both failed to convey the experience and underlying emotion— the impact of the Kennedy assassination and ensuing events— in a voice and manner I was comfortable with; that I felt was mine. None of my fictional forays ever did. The essay has.

I did write a short poem. After finishing a rough draft, I tried intermingling parts of it with the other pieces I was working on for *A*

Ballad of the '60s. I added several other lines, eventually discarded them. Finally, I left what I'd done as is. The poem never had a title. It was the only thing I finished while in San Francisco. In retrospect, maybe it was the only thing I needed to. The poem goes:

Lazy Indian summer quivers as coppers, auburns, and tans plummet to earth... then disappear in dismal, dreary winds of bare November.

Death enters serenely. Opiate scent wandering and twisting through chill air to intoxicate and soothe. Sun time shortened by lengthening darkness... life spends itself in October slumber before whirling unexpectedly into winter touches. It, too, falls gently to earth.

Death stalks... tiger in search of prey... Misty white shroud blowing in from the north woods... turning ragged expression into pale lifeless cold.

Death strikes... rattler's lightening quick bite... Slowly numbing as it rushes through the blood-soaked veins... red brilliant glow dazzling the western sky... last rays of light shadow into breathless night.

Life enters... drifting like a phantom through the gloomy night... lonely rider upon the wasteland. Orange streaks over the foggy eastern shore, pierces through this soft parade of summer smoke... in the distance was the light of home.

***

Two days before the Thanksgiving holiday I boarded a plane in San Francisco, and returned to mid-Michigan.

The echoes of November... of sadness, regret, and failed hopes... but also of laughter, many blessings, and maybe a few accomplishments. They blend together, ghost-like shadows of memory that span the years. They keep me company as I move along; a rider upon this land, traveling through these fleeting moments alongside family and friends, writing my ballads.

At the Straits of Mackinac

The park bench I'm sitting on rests only a few feet from the shoreline of Lake Huron, near the southern end of Mackinac Bridge. Close by is the rebuilt Fort Michilimackinac, an inviting place for tourists (like us) to examine and, by doing so, possibly discern some history. Off in the distance, beyond these straits where two of the Great Lakes meet, I can see the hazy landscape of the Upper Peninsula and of Mackinac Island.

I like this spot despite its popularity with other sightseers. The folks here are well-behaved and do not cause too much distraction.

Today the lake is choppy from a stiff breeze. Small whitecaps come rolling towards us from the northwest, wave after wave swooshing upon the beach, and then retreating back to the sea. This rhythm and repetition of sound and motion have gone on for thousands and thousands of summer afternoons. For a few moments, we witness the ebb and flow.

Pebbles litter this shoreline and my nine-year-old son picks several up and tosses them into the waters. Will these stones remain there? Or will they one day return to the beach, only to be thrown back by another youngster? Such activity must be instinctual. Most of us have the impulse. Are we challenging the enormity of nature? A stone and a human appear insignificant when juxtaposed against the broad horizon and immense volume of these fresh-water seas.

By throwing the pebbles into the waters are we simply doing our part to rearrange the scene, like a bird picking up a stray twig to fashion a nest? Is this activity another thin strand in the ecological web? Or are we just restless, needing more to do than stand and look?

The fort, the bridge, and the small city around this park are testimony that "we", past and present, have done much more than toss stones into the waters, although I imagine a fair number have gone sailing through the air over the years. A Visitor Center, underneath the bridge and only a few feet away, functions as a gift shop, selling historical books on this area along with related knick knacks and souvenirs. The shop also serves as the admission entrance to the fort. A plaque outside the center reads in part:

"Fort Michilimackinac (1715-1781) is one of hundreds, perhaps thousands, of colonial settlements built in North America, South America, Asia and Africa, whose purpose it was to control the region for the mother country.

"Michilimackinac served as a fur center, an embassy to Native Americans, a fortified town in French times, a military fort in British times, and a place from which exploration and military expeditions took place."

The British abandoned this fort on the tip of Michigan's mitten during the American Revolution in favor of a more strategically positioned, defensible outpost on the high bluff of Mackinac Island.

The plaque noted that "the remains of similar colonial forts, such as Pontchartrain at Detroit, Duquesne at Pittsburgh and San Carlos at St. Louis have long since disappeared with the building of modern cities." Because of this locale's previous remoteness, the dirt-covered remains of Michilimackinac, were largely intact when archaeologists began their diggings at the site in 1959. The artifacts they've discovered and put on display, coupled with the live reenactments of 18th century life in the settlement and the reconstructed palisade and buildings, are what's offered to visitors.

While the fort is now a curiosity (its practical mission having ended long ago), the Mackinac Bridge serves both of those purposes. The bridge's importance has been evident since it opened in November 1957. Sometime this summer, the 100th million vehicle will drive across it. Last year alone, 4.6 million vehicles used it. Still, the 'Mighty Mac' is as much a grand sight as a vital transportation link. At this bench where I relax, you can hear the low rumble of automobiles and semis coming onto or leaving the bridge. Normally such noise is intrusive. However, the sound and sight of the traffic moving along the five-mile arc seems an essential aspect of the scenic view.

The cars and trucks, looking more like toys than high-powered machines as they creep between the 552-foot twin towers, lend a proper perspective to this man-made marvel: a feat of engineering and construction that was mighty in its conception, and in its subsequent achievement. It is a testament to ambitions that begin as aspirations and are realized with a 'can do' ingenuity.

For now, the bridge stands tall, seemingly sturdy and durable; a monument rising above the waves of the Straits of Mackinac. But these pebbles that were once rock tell of nature's relentless power, while the fort reminds us of the changes that both time and our evolving ingenuity bring.

The Morning Rain

August 1998— I hum the lyrics from the Gordon Lightfoot song about "the early morning rain" as I watch the mist fall gently on this summer morning. I am sitting under the small awning of our pop-up camper, protected from the elements as I drink a cup of coffee. My wife and son are still inside, not quite ready to launch a new day.

The falling rain is not an unpleasant situation. At least not yet. Wet conditions do indeed dampen much of the fun and maneuverability of camping, limiting one's options. This adverse weather, however, has created a tranquil setting, muting the usual hustle and bustle that greets the awakening hours at a crowded campground. Soon, all too soon, an uproar of kids riding their bikes or gliding along on their roller blades, moms scolding their offspring, dogs barking, and dads grumbling about all of the racket will fill the air.

A few moments of quiet are to be savored. The start of our three-and-a-half-day vacation here at the Gun Lake Campground has, up until now, been blessed with splendid weather despite a dire forecast of thunderstorms. Sunny skies and a stirring breeze proved an optimal mix for our first-day excursion to the nearby beach. I managed to gradually wade out into the lake without too much difficulty; the shock of cold water against my skin is not a favorite sensation.

Once immersed in the water, I did a bit of thrashing around, charitably called swimming. After this quick exercise was out-of-the way, I got on the floating tube and spent the next half-hour bobbing about on top of the mild waves. Then I returned to shore and relaxed in my beach chair. "It's the posh, posh camping life for me," I sing to myself.

Bradley, meanwhile, waded into the water closer to shore, using his inner tube, only a few yards away from his ever-vigilant mother. Afterwards, he dug up some wet sand and then bugged me for money to buy fries at the concession stand. I pointed out that we'd eaten breakfast only a couple of hours before. He persisted on his needing food to quell the pangs of hunger. An easy touch, I hand him two dollars. Fries are not cheap at the park's beachfront store.

Later, after swimming, we had lunch at a restaurant on the other side of the lake, the Circle Inn. Bradley ordered chicken strips, Dawn had a sandwich and salad, while I requested a platter of frog legs. The last time I ate at this place was on Easter Sunday. My wife and son were enjoying spring vacation in Arizona, visiting her brother and sister-in-law, as well as others from that branch of the family who live there and also seeing the sights. I had remained in Michigan, attempting to keep the newspaper operating as best I could without my two bosses around.

Mom and my step-dad, Bob, invited me out for Easter dinner. I had previously told my mother about this restaurant, informing her that the place served frog legs, one of her favorite meals. She suggested we go there that Sunday. This occasion turned out to be the final opportunity we had to dine out together.

As I sit here at the campsite, it's been five weeks since we lost Mom. Her long illness, initially Lupus and then diabetes, with its sundry of deteriorating consequences, finally proved too much. What seemed only a moment ago— her death and then the funeral— is gradually, day by day, receding into the distance. We experience the vivid, sharp emotion— our grief— that the death of a loved one causes. But it, too, goes by. Yet, the sadness and melancholy of loss never completely fades away. Traces remain. At times the sharpness returns, even after many years. These reminders are fortunate though because, it seems to me, if one cannot mourn our lost loved ones every so often, even after many years, then what is the worth of life? Or of the time we spent together? A few tears shed every now and then seem a fitting tribute to those who have preceded us.

In her healthier days Mom and Bob camped a lot. They liked having the family (mainly the grandkids) around when they did so. During recent summers, we shared a number of these outings with them. She'd be here now, joining us on this weekend excursion, if ill health had not taken her from us. I can hear her now, fretting about the possible poor weather, making preparations for our breakfast, perhaps recalling the dancing flames of the previous night's campfire, and maybe suggesting we drive over to the restaurant later in the day to order a plate of frog legs. But time goes by, and so must we.

So, I sit here on this early morning, looking out at the campground. I watch the rain as it falls gently, gently falling on all of us, the living and the dead.

On Sinatra & Song

In Australia, the "Aboriginal Creation myths tell of the legendary totemic beings who emerged from the ground and then wandered over the continent in Dreamtime, naming everything that crossed their path — birds, animals, plants, rocks, waterholes, and so brought the world into existence." Writing about this in his fascinating book *The Songlines*, the late Bruce Chatwin suggests that these first beings sang the world into existence. In supporting this contention, he noted that each Australian native— as part of their belief system— memorizes a specific song that was sung by the totemic being (or sacred ancestor) from which he or she is descended. This song describes a linear path from one location to another; a path that a tribe of wandering hunters and gatherers would take. The lyrics and rhythm of the musical notes detail the physical highlights found along the route, including rises and dips in the landscape, mountain ranges, rivers, where water can be found in the desert, the flora and fauna, noticeable landmarks, and the location of sacred sites.

The songs, Chatwin explained, served as a way of passing vital information from one generation to another, as a form of trade (one person exchanging his song, i.e. knowledge of the land with others), and as a means for the different wandering bands to mark out both their territory and shared places (usually water holes).

These musical roadmaps, Chatwin speculated, were originally tools of survival for early mankind in a harsh environment, and that their usage predated the Aboriginals' emigration to Australia from Asia. He felt, as well, that the Songlines later evolved into a tool of social organization.

The subject is more complex than this, however. An essential point he makes is that historically and perhaps innately humans use songs to define themselves, the world around them, and as guides in navigating the treacherous terrain of life and living. Some scholars contend that our first utterances were a musical sing-song which led to language, not the reverse.

Whether this is true or not, there's no doubt that the use of song to explain and enhance goes way back. "Sing, O daughter of Zion; shout, O Israel!" reads the verse in the Old Testament book of Zephaniah. "Be glad and rejoice with all the heart, O daughter of Jerusalem!"

In the Christian Hymn Festival *We Sing Our Faith*, the beginning narrative echoes the Aboriginal myth. It goes: "All God's children have a place in the choir because God wants us to sing. And what do we sing? We sing our story, our song of freedom, life and healing through God's gift of saving grace.

"Singing hymns, singing our faith, is one of the few things people actively do together anymore. Singing hymns is among the last vestiges in our culture of the kind of communal activities that kept societies together since the dawn of history...," it continues. "One reason people gather to sing is instinctual. We have to sing together to know who we are."

Song, perhaps, even spawned Western literature. The epic poem of Homer's *Iliad*— the story of the great warrior Achilles and the Greek siege of Troy— begins:

"Achilles' wrath, to Greece the direful spring
Of woes unnumber'd heavenly goddess, sing!"

The above comments might seem an odd preamble for discussing Frank Sinatra who recently (in May 1998) died at age 82. It's done to emphasize the key role song has played, and still does, in our human relationships and in our inner beings.

Much has been told of Sinatra's vibrant life; his impact as an entertainer and celebrity during a nearly 60-year career and his legacy, including the many successes and the well-chronicled controversies. But at the core of those various discourses was a respect for and tribute to his singing abilities, the way he celebrated song, the influence his interpretative vocalizing had on American popular music and the larger culture, and how his synthesis of singing and lifestyle helped frame his generation's outlook on life and living.

Sinatra's music possessed range and depth: it was brassy and sentimental, hard-edged and vulnerable, casual, yet consummately professional; part traditional and part innovative; upbeat, soulful, reflective and sure-footed. He served up the familiar standards during his concerts, although he liked to improvise by slightly altering the lyrics and melodies. Yet, as any study of his recording catalog shows, he was open to new musical genres and to new, different approaches and styles.

During his career he collaborated with everyone from Tommy Dorsey to Nelson Riddle, from Duke Ellington to Antonia Carolos Jobim, and in his later year with younger rock stars. He cut his teeth on big band swing and romantic crooning. While maintaining this foundation, he later did jazz, basa nova, pop, and (most effectively) what he called 'saloon songs'— those intimate, sad torch poems of loss and longing.

In my younger days, while in college and for a few years after, I devoured Sinatra's music. I wanted to write stories the way he sang lyrics. Many singers and writers, I told anyone willing to listen, find a style, then they tend to mold the song or story to fit it. Even though they might possess a nice or arresting manner, this ultimately becomes limiting.

Sinatra, I felt, treated each piece he did with integrity. He tailored his voice and interpretation to include the intentions of the composer (or arranger) as well as the talents of the musicians accompanying him. He still maintained a recognizable personal style and approach. Every artist should do so. The difference is that he used his talent— the confidence he had in it— to showcase the songs rather than his singing style.

As a writer, I believed (and still do) that each story, person profiled, or topic of consideration should be treated in the same fashion. You needn't submerge your flair or voice, but neither should the technique of style overwhelm the contents nor distract the reader from the main focus.

If each writing project is given that integrity, then over time, and with effort, the reward is a repertoire that helps us better understand *who we are;* this life we have, what we believe in, and what we long for.

The journey has served as our culture's great metaphor of life. If songs were once descriptions of the physical habitat and spiritual landmarks of our pathways, they remain so "in a sense."

Sinatra, with his songs, first told of youth, promise and romance — all etched in the dark hues and urgency of war. Later, his music would reflect on personal setbacks and heartbreaks, and the determination to rebound from them. He sang of the joys of fatherhood. He also celebrated the full flower of robust adulthood, maybe too robustly at times. Eventually, there would be the retrospection of the *September Years,* a blend of loneliness, defiance, and resignation; yet also of fullness.

Finally, there arrived the aging maturity that combined past triumphs and a richness of experience with the lingering desire to mount new challenges. And mount them he did. Never having rested on his musical laurels, his last popular recordings were *Duets*, done with a variety of younger singers.

Sinatra was the premier balladeer of his generation. His songs touched them, influenced them, and helped define their journey. He leaves behind a pathway of song that others, now and in future years, can follow.

This Business of Horses

"There is something about the outside of a horse that is good for the inside of a man."

... One of the speakers used this line during the funeral eulogy of Merlin 'Doc' Eggleston in October 1999. A veterinarian by trade, Doc also trained draft horse teams on his Fowlerville farm for pulling competition. I learned later that the sentiment came from Winston Churchill

* * *

With faith in that testimony and the promise it holds, this past winter we bought a horse for our son, Bradley. Or more accurately, we adopted one. Along with the grandkids and our cat, she's now a part of the family.

Her name is Bobbie Socks Fever... Bobbie for short. She's a registered quarter horse, chestnut-colored, with a white blaze forehead, white socks on her forelegs, and a small strip of white hair at the root of her tail— a sort of beauty mark. She stands about 15 hands high (five feet), although— perhaps like a lineman's listed weight in a football program— this measurement may be a tad high. No matter. Like the porridge in *Goldilocks*, she's "just right".

Bobbie was born on May 31, 1984 in Gobles, a small town northwest of Kalamazoo, making her 16 years old this week. According to her registration papers, she did a bit of moving about in her younger days. After Gobles there were stops in two Ohio towns, then back to Michigan for stays in Jasper, Adrian, and Haslett.

It was in the summer of 1993 that the Leggett family of Dimondale brought her to their small country farm, and there Bobbie came under the pampering care of middle daughter, Sara, who was 11 years old and in 4-H.

And it's as a 4-H horse that we now use her. Bradley, who's coincidently 11 years old, has joined that esteemed organization. His club is called 'Bridles & Bits.' As the late western writer Louis L'Amour would say, "We now ride for that brand."

Since she arrived at the stable where we board her, Bobbie and Bradley have spent many hours getting acquainted. A quiet and unassuming lady, she has for the most part allowed her young rider, without too much fuss or protest, to complete his initial lessons in horsemanship.

She did test us a couple of weeks after we got her (as we learned horses are prone to do when dealing with new riders), including two half-hearted bucks and some nips. To Bradley's credit, he didn't become frighten and quit. Bobbie, being basically a gentle critter, soon abandoned that strategy and resumed her mannerly behavior.

She has also patiently put up with Bradley's two assistants, his mom and dad, despite our having made a few stumbles and mistakes along the way. Fortunately, our lack of experience concerning this business of horses has been offset by the advice and generous help of others (the owners and fellow boarders) at the stable. Without those helping hands, I'd still be trying to figure out the proper method for putting on the bridle: One evening during our first week as horsemen, I put it on cock-eyed three straight times. Poor Bobbie must have wondered why I kept pushing the bit into her mouth and then almost immediately taking it out.

But we're slowly getting the hang of things. The routine has become a familiar one. First, we fetch the mare from the paddock, and then we groom her, clean the hooves, and put on the saddle and bridle. After that Bradley rides her. When finished, we brush her down, give her a treat, and return her to the pasture.

Since she's at a stable, we're not responsible for the assorted duties that come with operating a livestock barn, primarily feeding the animals and cleaning the stalls. But we try to pitch in where and when the situation arises, both as a "thank you" for favors rendered, and because it's what you do when hanging around a barn. From time to time we've swept the alleyway, filled the water buckets, pushed the hay cart, and removed the errant pile of manure when it appears. Even my city-girl wife (ever the good sport) is becoming proficient in the use of a fork and wheelbarrow to remove those inevitable droppings.

In recent weeks there have been riding lessons at the stable, workouts with the 4-H club at the fairgrounds, 4-H club meetings, re-wiring the old horse trailer I purchased, and frequent trips to the tack store. When we first mentioned this decision to get a horse, the suggestion from old hands in the business was for us to order an extra box of checks: in other words to be prepared to spend some money. Unlike many tips and prophecies one hears over a lifetime, this advice has proven accurate. Purchasing the necessary equipment and horse-care accessories, outfitting Bradley in the appropriate attire, paying for the riding instructor and farrier, and covering the assorted 4-H fees have seemed as costly and never-ending as operating a weekly newspaper. Thus far, we've managed to "grin and bear it;" a stoic reaction that may indeed be due to our having become accustomed (or immune) to the "sticker shock" that comes with owning a business, especially at tax time.

But all kidding aside, I view the horse and all that goes with her as an investment. While I would not mind one day amassing a modest fortune, I figure (as the old cliché tells us) that "you can't take it with you." And, on a more personal level, I figure that "you only live once," and 11-year-olds all too soon become 21-year-olds. Certain opportunities, if not taken, can slip forever away.

Watching Bradley sitting atop Bobbie as they jog around the riding arena is worth giving up a few luxuries during the retirement years. Besides, there are (I hope) life lessons being offered here that will go beyond any dollar calculation. I hope my son will learn to be responsible and fulfill his obligations. Further, that he will discover the importance of attending to details and of practicing; and that he will know the virtue of being patient and develop the fortitude to deal with and overcome setbacks. When all is said and done, I believe he will see that this mixture of work and fun brings rewards of personal satisfaction and accomplishment.

There are, I'm confident, adventures and new paths awaiting him during these upcoming 4-H years that, likewise, go beyond any financial measurement. He'll make new friends, visit interesting places, and experience a wide range of memorable moments.

Still, having stated all of that, this business of horses is not, I confess, entirely about my son. As a former farm boy who now resides in town, spends many hours at a desk, and peddles papers for a livelihood, I had an urge to get back to the amenities of a barn and rural scenery; back to alfalfa, cobwebs, wooden fences, and the rest. I wanted to do more than simply remember and reminisce about a long-ago country past. I wished to instead regain, even in a small way, the tasks of caring for an animal and the routine of barn work. While the distance between the dairy farm of my youth and a horse stable may seem far, and maybe the comparison is a bit farfetched, this endeavor seems a chance to re-connect this stage of life with that earlier one. And to show my son, in a small way, what my past was like.

Perhaps all of this may seem a pretty heavy load of expectation for a small 16-year-old mare to carry… to take a young boy into his future, and an aging fellow back to his rural roots. But I think Bobbie Socks Fever is just the horse to get us there.

At the End of a Fair Week

On this early morning, as I walk across the campgrounds of the fair, I hear the loud squeal of a hog as he's being loaded onto a livestock truck. A mournful sound to my mind, but mournful only because I know his destination on this fine Sunday will be the butcher's shop.

As for the hog, the prodding and poking as he's pushed up the ramp and into the truck is more of an annoyance and uncertainty. He possesses no foreknowledge of his impending fate, though soon enough he'll sense that things have gone haywire in his heretofore leisurely life. A sad end for a critter that had been primed and pampered all week at the fair (and in the months leading up to it), but agriculture— this livelihood that puts food on the nation's table— is by necessity a hard-eyed business.

My own destination at this fresh hour, with the grass still wet from the heavy dew, is the horse barn. A few, like me, are up and about, while others (more sensible) have not yet stirred from their tents and campers.

While the fair had ended officially the night before, our 4-H horse Bobbie still needs to be fed and watered. Then there remains the task of removing the sawdust bedding and wiping down the stall with water and bleach before we all head for home. Unlike the hog and other market livestock, she receives a happier end to fair week. Bobbie and many of the other horses, along with the dairy cows, carnival barkers and the rest of the cast and characters (our family included) will, Lord willing, be back next summer for a return engagement.

The fair, only a few hours before, was bursting with nocturnal energy and activity; vibrant with its unique sensation of sights, sounds and smells, blending gaudy show business, neon lights, and fried foods in the same venue with the culture of the farm. On this morning after, the place has a subdued and forlorn look.

Nearly all of the midway rides and games, which the operators started tearing down at the stroke of midnight, have packed up and left for the next destination. Their bright and colorful lights, loud background music, striped awnings, and stuffed-animal prizes have become memory. The concessionaire wagons have also closed up and are now preparing to depart. A goodly number of exhibit animals—the horses and dairy cows—have, likewise, taken off.

What remains, besides us stragglers and our animals, are bags of trash stacked next to overflowing barrels, and paper cups and wrappers that lay scattered about the grounds. The mess will keep the clean-up crew busy. Also needing to be removed or stored away are piles of manure near the barns, and a multitude of signs, stalls, cages, tables, chairs, tents and other accessories.

Only one week before, all the hundreds of pieces that comprise a fair— people, show animals, arts & crafts, merchandise, food concessions, midway rides, electric cables, animal cages, stalls, tents, banners, ticket rolls, pitch forks, PA systems, tractors, hay, sawdust, and more— had come together to create this mid-summer festival. Now the dispersal is underway, not nearly as exciting or motivating of an occasion. The adrenaline of anticipation had long ago been spent.

At both the start and finish, as well as throughout the week, there was the appearance of chaos: a moving mosaic of dozens of people doing this and that, seemingly without direction. But what guided that mishmash of flurry and scurry was the pattern of past experience, along with a knowledge possessed by many people of how the pieces fit together and how the different activities should function and occur. Further helping to guide matters are the established rules, the planned organization, and tradition.

The veteran fair participants know where to go and what to do. Newcomers need mainly to ask questions, and follow the experienced folks' lead as much as possible; although neither questioning nor following are guarantees that you won't get a little confused, miss out on something, or make a wrong step.

While we can't claim to be total novices, having been to and taken part in other fair weeks over the years, those involvements were in other capacities. This was our first time out as a 4-H family, taking part in club activities, and of tending to and showing a horse.

"Volunteers are the heart of the fair," Tom Braun told me nearly 24 years ago during a newspaper interview. Tom, who was the secretary of the Fowlerville Fair at the time, stressed that it was all those dozens of folks, serving and helping out in a myriad of ways, who created the vim and vigor, and who pumped the necessary life's blood into this rural institution. He added that these dedicated, unselfish, and hard workers are the ones who make a fair happen, and who sustain it over the long haul.

Although I'd be hard-pressed to qualify for those superlatives, I tried as a brand-new 4-H father to take that observation "to heart," and assist where and how I could. I sought to learn as much as possible from the veteran 4-Hers.

Our initial outing proved most enjoyable. Bobbie behaved splendidly, perhaps partly because we bribed her with more hay than her usual allotment. In appreciation, she gave us plenty of opportunities to clean out the stall. Show day proved hectic and tiring, with a good deal of brushing and polishing, and general fussing, but Bradley and Bobbie performed well. The two of them earned a few ribbons to tack up on the stall door. Bradley also did well with the ink drawing and photographs he entered.

More importantly, we got acquainted with other families in the club. There was also time during the week to examine the other animals: dairy and beef cattle, goats and woolly-headed sheep, rabbits, poultry, and swine. One evening, I watched the pen-of-hogs competition, a rather entertaining spectacle. How a judge can keep a ring full of scampering pigs straight in his head is beyond me, but he did just that.

Another night we watched a rodeo; and still another, I paid a dollar to milk an Alpine goat. I found the goat much easier to milk (by hand) than a Holstein cow, although I have no desire to do either on a regular basis. I learned long ago, having grown up on a dairy farm, that milk animals bind you close to home. Having to milk them twice a day is an obligation that allows few opportunities to roam too far away for too long.

On this final morning, with all those experiences now behind us, as we feed Bobbie and begin the clean-up, I am ready for the fair to be over, yet still a little wistful.

Like countless other parents who've come before us, we brought our boy and his horse here. We were a small part in a much larger event. When we finally leave the grounds, we'll be taking home much more than we brought. For this I feel grateful. But sad, too, for I realize, as a 4-H family, we will never come here again for the first time. We'll never again get to experience and enjoy the fair from that fresh perspective.

Visiting the Gerald R. Ford Presidential Museum

On a week when Vice President Al Gore and Gov. George W. Bush battled for the Presidency in the courthouses of Florida… When we learned all about "pregnant" chads— the term given when the small rectangle in a punch-card ballot (called a chad) is indented, but not punched through— and we learned all about their cousins, the "swinging" chads— the term used when the hole is punctured, but the pesky chad still hangs on for dear life by a corner or two…When man, once the measure of all things, was asked to bend knee and defer to the ultimate, almighty authority of the computerized machine… One day during that week I took my 12-year-old son to visit the Gerald R. Ford Museum in Grand Rapids.

Upon entering the front doors, you see an excerpt from the brief remarks Ford made after taking the oath of President on August 9, 1974, shortly after he and others had seen Richard Nixon depart the White House, his letter of resignation already submitted.

"I am acutely aware," Ford said on that distant day, "that you have not elected me as your President by your ballots, and so I ask you to confirm me as your President with your prayers. And I hope that such prayers will also be the first of many."

The museum is rich in details and artifacts of Gerald Ford's life and public-service career. More information exists here than one can ever summarize in a newspaper column. What you learn, with this collection, is the path that one man took— a direction pursued partly by choice, ambition and hard work and partly by chance. And you see how this personal journey intersected with historical destiny.

Gerald Ford reached that time and place by the route of who he was and what he'd done (a mix of character, fortitude and effort). Coinciding with this was a host of circumstances beyond his doing or control that likewise made him President.

The assorted events and outcomes of the Watergate Break-in and Cover-up were, of course, the most prominent of these circumstances. In June of 1972, five men (members of the Nixon Re-election Committee) were caught burglarizing the Democratic Party offices located in the Watergate Hotel in Washington, D.C. The chain reaction that this criminal act of political espionage set off would eventually have a major impact on both the nation and one of its citizens— a Republican Congressman of 25 years from Western Michigan.

Viewing the unfolding narrative of Watergate— shown with words, pictures, and artifacts— brought back assorted memories, many of them half-forgotten after over a quarter of a century. The chronology possesses, in retrospect, a panoramic quality: so many players, episodes, happenstances, and unforeseen repercussions. For my young son, none of this held any personal connection. Still, as a father, you sow the seeds with this visit, trust a few of them will sprout and grow, and that one day they will provide a harvest.

The museum obviously includes highlights of the Ford Administration— the major issues and events of this brief presidency. Also on display is information about the two assassination attempts. And there are details of the 1976 election, held during the country's bi-centennial year. That campaign saw the conservative Ronald Reagan challenge the more moderate Ford for the GOP nomination. Afterwards, it became a race to the finish line, with Ford rallying from a 22-point deficit in the polls after the Republican Convention to nearly overtake Jimmy Carter by Election Day. However, with strong support in the South, Carter won with 297 electoral votes to Ford's 240 and captured 40.8 million popular votes to Ford's 39.1 million total.

What I found of greater interest, though, was the story of Gerald Ford's youth— as a boy and then as a young man— a narrative of family events and various choices that shaped him and finally launched him upon this road of destiny.

His mother Dorothy, with a baby in tow, left an abusive husband in Nebraska and relocated in Grand Rapids. There she married Gerald R. Ford, Sr., who subsequently adopted the boy and gave him his name.

"In the Ford household three rules were absolute (for young Gerald and his three younger half-brothers)," notes one of the displays. "Tell the truth, work hard, and come to dinner on time."

He became an Eagle Scout. He attended South High School in Grand Rapids, joining a student body that included a diverse combination of Polish, Italian, and Black Americans (in contrast to the more elite and exclusionary schools in the community) and in 1930, his senior year, he played on South High's mythical state champion football team.

Ford then attended the University of Michigan and starred as a lineman on its football squad. An All-Big 10 selection his final season, he played in the Shiners' East-West All–Star game.

He turned down offers to play professional ball for the Detroit Lions and Green Bay Packers— certainly a financial temptation during those Depression years— and instead got his foot in the door at Yale Law School by coaching at the college and attending a few classes. After finally being accepted there, he graduated in 1941.

Returning to Grand Rapids, Ford and another attorney formed a partnership. But the start of this law firm was soon "scuttled" by the Japanese bombing of Pearl Harbor and America's entry into World War II. He joined the Navy, and later saw combat aboard the USS Monterey in the Pacific Theater. After the war ended, he again headed home and resumed practicing law. However, like many attorneys, he had his eye on politics and elective office.

The year 1948 proved a pivotal one for Ford. A museum display notes: "His war experiences taught him the importance of American involvement and leadership in world affairs." Hence, the young internationalist decided to take on the isolationist Republican incumbent in the 5th Congressional District primary. Receiving an important (and unexpected) endorsement from the *Grand Rapids Press*, the 35-year-old challenger won the nomination, was elected, and went on to be re-elected 12 more times.

As if running for office was not enough, in October of 1948 he and Betty were married. With his bride, he went off to the nation's capital. Another display tells us that he "earned an early reputation among his peers for hard work, steadiness and keeping his word." In 1964 he stepped out onto the national stage, where he would remain, by being selected as the House's Republican Minority Leader.

The museum narrative explains that Ford's dream was to serve as Speaker of the House. However, with the Democrats firmly in control of this Congressional body during those years and, thus, in charge of the legislative process, Gerald and wife Betty had agreed after the '72 election that he'd run one more time (in 1974) and then retire from Congress at the end of 1976.

But, as we now know, the dark storm clouds of Watergate were already building up along the horizon and would soon blow across the land, giving the Fords a profoundly different future then they had envisioned.

In October of 1973, Ford was designated by President Nixon to replace Spiro Agnew as vice president, Agnew having resigned office amid corruption charges that dated back to his Maryland governmental days. The House confirmed that selection on Dec. 6. Then, a little over eight months later, Nixon also resigned, and Ford took the oath as our 38th President.

One of the museum's exhibits suggests that Gerald Ford "would be called upon to bridge America's internal divisions— to heal her conflicts and restore her confidence."

Watergate was part of those divisions and conflicts. It came on the heels of and occurred as a result of other cultural and political clashes that had been going on during the late 1960s and early 1970s. The War in Vietnam with the hawks and doves, civil rights vs. states' rights, student unrest and law-and-order, the Silent Majority versus alternate lifestyles were all among the famous "gaps" that then existed.

I think from our current vantage point, we can indeed credit Ford's steady hand, his forthrightness, and his moderate temperament with having helped build this symbolic bridge that helped move us beyond those troubled times. We know that not everyone has wished to bridge those gaps or forgot the old grudges. And, we realize— given the current controversy over the 2000 Presidential Election— that there'll always be divisions, conflicts, and tests of confidence that we, as a nation and as citizens, must face and work through.

I left the Ford Museum with this lesson: At a moment of such reckoning, at a national fork-in-the-road, we were fortunate to find standing there a person of character and basic virtue. We were blessed by a man who, upon assuming the Presidency in those harsh and passionate times, chose to become a source of conciliation, not retribution; who served with grace and an unpretentious manner, rather than displaying an arrogant attitude. I think this character and attitude were properly reflected in Gerald Ford's final address to Congress, given on Jan. 12, 1977 as he was about to leave that high office.

"My fellow Americans, I once asked you for your prayers, and now I give you mine: May God guide this wonderful country, its people and those they have chosen to lead them. May our third century be illuminated by liberty and blessed with brotherhood, so that we, and all who come after us, may be the humble servants of thy peace."

A Walk in the Park

This area of the park where I now walk is relatively quiet. Only a background hum of indistinguishable sounds can be heard. I seem to have the place to myself of this late autumn afternoon. That's a far cry from the summer months when dozens of swimmers, boaters, picnickers and sight-seers flock here on a daily basis.

Now the beach is deserted. The pavilion, with its restrooms and coin-operated food concessions, has been locked up until next spring. The nearby playground finds only a couple of black squirrels scurrying around, in place of the children who only recently frolicked on the swings and slide, and rode on the merry-go-round.

The day, itself, is not an encouraging one for outdoor enthusiasts. But I do not mind it, nor the apparent solitude. A cold breeze hints at approaching winter; the ground is still damp from recent rains, while the sky, with its bluish-gray overcast, seems hard-edged.

This park, which neighbors a state campground, is located on a narrow peninsula that juts out into Gun Lake. The waters to the west, normally picturesque and inviting, mirror the gloomy sky overhead. Steel-blue and foreboding, the wind ripples the surface. Only the far shore of houses and trees— indistinct in the distance, the foliage a hazy mixture of green, yellow, scarlet, and dull browns— mar this scene of "blue above blue."

Conversely, the small, protected cove on the east side of the peninsula appears tranquil. A more benign blend of light and dark reflects off the lake's surface, while the row of homes and trees along the opposing shore, more vivid in detail and color, resembles an autumn postcard.

I soon hear the sound of machinery elsewhere in the park, so I'm not entirely alone. A little more walking and I spot the tall arm of a crane above the tree line, then a barge anchored at the water's edge. Some kind of project's underway. I decide to investigate. As I climb the hill that overlooks the beach area, with this more advantageous view, I see an earthmover: the actual source of the sound I've been hearing, going back and forth, smoothing out a pile of dirt and blending it with the fill sand.

The work site is next to an existing boat launch and parking lot. It's quickly apparent that a second, duplicate parking area is being prepared with the asphalt crew only a few days away.

What the crane and barrage are doing, I'm unsure. At first I figure a second boat launch is being constructed and that the location is being readied for a concrete pour. Later, though, after asking a park ranger, I learn that the barge and crane were used to dredge the channel between the campground and park. “That’s where the fill sand came from,” he said.

“There was already a parking lot there to handle the overflow,” he noted. “But it was gravel and kind of hodge-podge. They had some money in the boating fund (user fees collected from boat licenses) to do something, so they decided to pave it.”

Having been here during the summer, I can understand the need. The current launch, setting on the eastern shore of the peninsula and facing the cove, gets overcrowded during the warm-weather weekends. A long line-up of autos and trailers often forms as folks wait to unload or load their assorted craft. The existing paved lot is quickly filled, with others (arriving later) parking wherever space allows. This second improved lot, blacktopped with white markings, should provide more order on those crowded days, and get the maximum benefit out of the space.

Were park officials to ever decide to build a second launch, it would (at least temporarily) help alleviate the line-up problem. That, in turn, would be good news for those needing to utilize a public access to enjoy the lake. But I’m pretty sure this sort of project would not be welcome news for the property owners who must share these waters with an already large flotilla of boaters on summer Saturdays and Sundays. These visitors range from the speed demons in their high-powered cigar boats to the proliferating jet skiers to the aging baby boomers who increasingly favor the comforts of a pontoon.

I’m of two minds about creating more access, thus encouraging more boaters. The amenities of this or any place are diminished when too many try to squeeze onto or otherwise share a limited piece of geography. Additionally, with swimming, fishing, and quiet contemplation being other desired uses of this natural setting, the noise and numbers tend to overwhelm and dominate.

That being said, this resource should never be the exclusive domain of those who reside here. Equally to blame for the crowded conditions has been overdevelopment. Too many homes have been shoe-horned next to each other over the years, squeezed into every nook and cranny of shoreline, or along one of several channels that were dug so that additional lake-access building sites could be peddled. Those lined up at the public park, waiting their turn at the launch, have an equal right to enjoy this recreational activity.

What’s happened, of course, is that years ago a guy might buy a modest-sized row boat (with an outboard motor) that he could trailer around from fishing hole to fishing hole, but most of those who owned the larger pleasure craft did live on a lake…usually a seasonal cottage.

But that's certainly no longer the case. Our more affluent, leisure-seeking society— thanks to the easy credit payment system and a more ambitious appetite towards these recreational opportunities— has resulted in a lot of boat owners. Drive along any street or highway and you'll see them parked in driveways or on the side of the garage, with nearly all of them dependent on a public access site.

And those seasonal cottages have been converted and enlarged into year-round residences with the owners having a boat or two parked at the dock.

PARK ESTABLISHED IN MID-1930's

Having seen what was going on, I circle back, traipsing through the leaves that litter the ground. This park and the nearby campground are part of the 5,000-acre Yankee Springs Recreation Area. The history of the region and the Rec Area is an interesting one, the latter the result of both personal and national vision.

Harold Foster, the Barry County Agricultural agent in the 1930s, was the person most responsible for initiating the effort, but it was done within the context of President Franklin Roosevelt's overall effort to end the Great Depression and put Americans back to work.

Foster, in a report he gave back then on this project, stated:

"The Yankee Springs area was the first part of Barry County to be settled. It is on the old Grand Rapids-Kalamazoo (Indian) trail. It also borders the Thornapple River where the first trading posts were located. The soil for the most part is sandy; other soil is poor, gravelly loam soil.

"Both the sand and gravel are rough with quick steep slopes as well as long general hills. The sandy area of the territory was easily cleared of forests for farming. At the time it was fertile with years of leaf mulch, etc. (However) Due to the sandy, rolling nature, this soil did not last."

By the turn-of-the-century, much of the farming had become hard-scrabble. When Foster came to the county in 1930, during the dark early days of the Depression, "it was a very poor agricultural area." A sizable portion of property in this area had reverted back to the State of Michigan due to delinquent taxes. Also by 1930, hundreds of acres had gone out of production. Some of the farmsteads had been abandoned, while others had severely deteriorated, and a good amount of land (due to neglect or by choice) had returned to trees and brush.

The Ag agent initially looked for ways to improve agricultural productivity, but noted in his report that many landowners were not particularly interested. "In looking the whole thing over, I concluded the area to be worth far more as a woods resort area than an agricultural one," he said.

Foster interested local civic and school groups in small reforestation projects. He also sponsored tours of the area, aimed at showing its recreational offerings and building the necessary support for his idea. Aware of New Deal programs that were being established, he contacted federal authorities about converting a large area of the county into a national forest. At the time, Foster noted, he was proposing that 40,000 acres be purchased for forestry and resort use.

Over the next two to three years his two-fold approach began to show results. While local residents helped plant saplings in small plots, and came to better understand the recreational potential, federal officials were studying the proposal and doing on-site investigations. A change in direction occurred after a man from the Parks Division of the U.S. Forestry Service, looking over the proposed area with its lakes, scenic hills, and different cover "came here with the idea of a forestry area and he left with the idea it would make a wonderful recreational area."

Foster noted that he had little trouble gaining the backing of local movers and shakers, since this alternative would have a larger and more immediate economic benefit for the area. He then informed the federal agency of this local support.

Property was optioned, including nice beaches on lakes. Foster, in a report to the county board of supervisors, stated, "The plans for development proposed three permanent camp sites to accommodate about 150 people each."

"Every camp is (to be located) in a good wooded area on a nice beach. The camp will include a central office, mess hall, recreational hall and sleeping cabins."

One of the camps would be for boys, another camp (at another lake) would be for girls, and the third one at Long Lake would be for general use.

"Also, a large tourist and camp site is to be arranged on the peninsula extending into Gun Lake. This will be open to the traveling public with tents and house cars (trailers). This spot has a natural sand beach second to none."

There remained a few obstacles and delays along the way, but by 1937 work had begun on one of the camps with the goal of opening it later that summer.

Similar efforts were underway on the eastern side of the state, and elsewhere in the country. A May 1937 newspaper story stated, "The Waterloo recreational demonstration project in Washtenaw and Jackson counties, and the Yankee Springs project in Barry County will be developed by the National Park Service with a view to their maximum use by this season. Emphasis will be placed on the use of the areas for camps, especially for underprivileged folks from nearby cities. Jackson, Ann Arbor and Detroit are the cities which will benefit most from the use of the Waterloo area, while Grand Rapids, Kalamazoo and Battle Creek will have easy access to the Yankee Springs region."

Later in the article it noted that the Michigan areas "are only two of 46 of these recreational projects now under development in 24 states. They are all located within a half day's round trip distance of 30 million people."

While making these organized camps and day-use facilities accessible to nearby urban populations stood as a main priority, another stated purpose was that they serve as wildlife sanctuaries. Improvements and expansions have, of course, taken place at Yankee Springs and other locales during the ensuing years. For example, a trail system was created that's used by hikers, cross country skiers, snowshoe enthusiasts, and even bikers and joggers. Other recreational areas were later developed in Michigan, and the federal government eventually turned over these lands to the Michigan Dept. of Natural Resources. It's an irreplaceable inheritance. Countless visitors from near and far have enjoyed the Yankee Springs Rec Area over the past 66 years… as they have the other ones across the nation.

But it is a legacy that has been, and continues to be, put at risk. Different visions are at play.

We hear often from critics who, in historical retrospect, find fault with Roosevelt's New Deal policies (and, by extension, the whole notion of proactive, innovative government programs used to address social problems). This criticism would, I assume, included this multi-faceted project that bought unproductive farm land, gave the hard-pressed farm families a chance to re-locate in better circumstances, converted infertile land back to forests and swale or developed it for recreational use, and sought to provide impoverished families in our cities with convenient and inexpensive opportunities to camp, swim, boat, hike and sit around the campfire. At the same time, this public works project gave unemployed men a paying job, and set aside protected areas for native wildlife.

We also hear from those who feel the federal government as well as the State of Michigan currently possesses too many holdings; that some of the acreage ought to be sold off and turned over to private development. This proposal usually gets pushed during tight budget times with the contention that these revenues will help alleviate the crunch. Underlying this viewpoint is the time-honored belief that the sole purpose of natural resources is to serve private enterprise, with the beneficiaries generally being a select few individuals who possess wealth and control the levers of power.

These recurring calls to sell off public lands (and turn the bounty of natural resources over to a select few) seem out-of-kilter given the growing use of these parks, forests, and waterways. The contention that the public owns too much land also seems refuted by the residential and commercial sprawl that has shrunk the available (private) refuges for wildlife. Countering this privatization push are the nature conservancies and land trusts that seek to save as many of the remaining wild places as possible, or to convert marginal farm land back to a more natural state. In addition, we see the efforts by agricultural groups and others to preserve farmland and open spaces. These adherents point out the long-term economic and quality-of-life benefits gained by maintaining our farms and fields as well as woodlots. They warn us, as well, of the dangers of putting present-day expediency and profit ahead of these longer-term considerations.

When we observe what over-development has done to Gun Lake, a shoreline of wall-to-wall houses, a second tier of homes behind them, with more on the way, and compare that outcome to this park and this recreation area created over 60 years ago in the depths of the Great Depression, the choice of visions is starkly evident.

With more and more people seeking to share a limited resource, we face a few challenges:

—To protect and maintain these public trusts,

—To address the difficult task of balancing the varying and often times conflicting uses of our public lands and waterways,

—To balance the right of public access with the reasonable and understandable expectations that neighboring private owners have of enjoying their home and property,

—To maintain protected wildlife sanctuaries (even making some of them off limits) as a vital part of our public lands and waters, and

—To enhance and enlarge this legacy for future generations.

At The Campfire

We got our first whiff this year of campfire smoke on a recent Saturday night. Grandpa Bob, having traded in his motor home for a new fifth-wheel trailer (and a new pickup for towing it), was understandably anxious to launch the rig.

He invited a pair of grandsons, Bradley and Andrew, to serve as shipmates on the maiden voyage. They received free grub and free bunks and plenty of liberty for agreeing to this tour-of-duty. Not a bad deal, but then grandkids often fare well on such excursions with the senior generation.

Since the campground is nearby, my wife loaded up the car with extra food and we drove over to do some evening picnicking, followed by marshmallow roasting.

The state park was nearly full. The usually warm weekend weather — always a pleasant surprise during our northern springs— had prompted many to jump-start their out-of-doors recreational pursuits. Back home I would not easily tolerate the dense concentration, having little appetite for the constant racket and close proximity of other lives. Like many others, I prefer a little elbow room.

Here, however, amid a small city of RVs and old-fashioned tents, I accept the situation, even enjoy it, but am aware of the irony that this crowded and noisy setting is considered a means of rest and relaxation while our (usually) more spacious homes and neighborhoods are equated with the daily grind of work and other obligations. Many of us eagerly leave that setting for this.

Like others at the park, our tiny band spent the twilight hours huddled about the burning wood. The kids were restless, eating and then deciding to take another spin down the paved roadway on their bikes. We, adults, stayed put, talking and munching and, at the same time, studying the dancing flames. We meditate, consciously or unconsciously, on the mystery and allure of fire.

It's an old custom we're taking part in. We are not so far removed from our ancestors' existence when a campfire and close proximity to others were essential to survival. There exists a romance about the lone traveler. The reality and practicality though, proven over the long centuries, is that we're better off in small, co-operative groups. The family in its various forms and extensions, and the community— tied together by blood, geography, and shared culture— are the elemental ones we've fashioned.

We learned long ago that a person, alone at night or alone in life, is a vulnerable creature.

Our evening at the campfire, bothered only by the need to move our chairs to avoid the curling smoke, is vastly different from another part of the world. I think of the Kosovar Albanians, forced by thugs from their homes and towns and packed earlier this spring— when the weather over there was less hospitable— into makeshift camps.

One report described the scene as "a nightmarish swamp of mud and rain and human waste" and noted that during the initial days of this forced evacuation "family members were losing (contact with) one another in the dark."

Often only short spans exist between a workable situation, a strained one, and an untenable one; between what's pleasant, what's merely tolerable, and what's nightmarish. These refugee camps, shown on the TV news and pictured in the daily papers, are not much different from this temporary settlement at the state park. What separates them, the difference between the workable and the nightmarish, is the correlation of population to natural and man-made support systems.

Too many people, with not enough food, causes starvation. The high-speed freeway, packed suddenly with too many cars, becomes a frustrating traffic jam. Too many students in the school building (more than it's designed to handle) results in packed classrooms and fewer educational opportunities. Even so, a certain concentration of people is needed to provide abundant food, dependable transportation routes, and that school opportunity.

The matter is perplexing. For example, our large cities serve as engines of economic activity and as centers of cultural creativity, yet are conversely hotbeds of disease and crime. How can the equation work or why does it fail to work? What is the right mix of population to these support systems? How do we maintain a workable, agreeable civilization that, at the same time, fits into the ecology of the larger natural world?

How do we span the distance from discord to harmony, from chaos to order, or is that notion, itself, a problem? We ponder these questions with ideas, theories and schemes; our thoughts, imagination, and beliefs fueling this desire to sustain and perpetuate. From such instinct and faith, we toss the chunks of wood into the crackling flames, enjoy the light and warmth and companionship, but notice as well the ashes from the burning wood swirling in the heated air above the dancing fire, and from there these remnants float gently off into the dark, cool shadows and fall to earth. From fire to ash, from light to dark, only a short span exists.

Tears for a Departed Friend

While the larger world prepared for New Year's 2000 and fretted (needlessly it turned out) about Y2K computer disasters, family and friends said "good bye" to Jim Campbell, a 60-year-old Fowlerville man who died unexpectedly on Dec. 27.

There is no easy time to lose a family member or close acquaintance, but the Christmas holiday season would certainly not be many people's first choice. And, as far as the hierarchy of disasters goes, personal sorrow trumps most others. His obituary, appearing in last week's newspaper, prepared by his widow, Joyce, noted that he "loved the land, was a farmer at heart, and loved John Deere tractors, woodcarving, and old people."

In my chats with him over the years, I can testify to his affection for the land and the art of farming. I learned also that he regarded his elderly friends as treasure troves of knowledge and insight about bygone days of rural life. It was those bygone days, I'd suggest, that held an over-arching fascination and allure for him. Jim was, perhaps, a fellow born a bit out of his time. While he lived a full and, I believe, rewarding life in this half century, touching many lives with his generous and open nature, I think he'd have absolutely thrived in that earlier era. Back then the countryside was liberally dotted with small farms of a 100 acres or less, with a man able to make a livelihood caring for a couple dozen dairy cows. As for the social scene, it was more centered on neighborhood and village activities.

"People don't neighbor the way they used to," he once said to me, a reference to a way of country living that once existed.

Born in 1939, Jim, as a young fellow, caught the tail end of that era before farmers were advised in the '50s "to get big or get out." Most of them eventually chose the latter course. He didn't grow up on a farm. The family— which included his folks, Ralph and Alice, and younger sisters Arlene, Colleen, and Pat— resided on Sharpe Road, just outside of town. His dad was an electrician. However, like a lot of young fellows did back then, he found employment as a hired man on a farm after school, on weekends, and during the summer.

I don't know for how long a period, but while he was in high school, and for a short period after he returned from military service, Jim worked for my father when we were farming on what's now known as the Eggleston Farm on North Fowlerville Road. The Campbells lived right around the corner and for a spell, as Jim would say… we did a lot of neighboring. I was a youngster back then— a preschooler when we arrived, and eight years old when we relocated to the farm on North Gregory Road. As such, my memories are mostly fragments of various incidents, events, and special occasions. Despite that lack of volume, there's a pervasive aura I feel about this long-ago time and place; one formed, I realize from early childhood experience (thus, possibly not overly accurate or realistic), yet none-the-less pleasant. Even magical. The world at that impressionable age can be the stuff of adventure and wide-eyed wonder.

Wandering through the croplands, exploring the pasture and woods that border the Red Cedar River on the back end of the place, racing quickly past the menacing bull pacing in its pen, dipping my hand into the cold water filled with milk cans, catching frogs, flying kites, discovering a huge puffball… those are only a few of the fragments.

Jim was an important part of that timeframe; his face and presence make up a significant part of my personal kaleidoscope. My dad died when he was 38. After I'd grown older, Jim served as a link to this period. Whenever we ran into each other and had a few moments to visit, I'd attempt to get him to reminisce about those days— something not too difficult to accomplish— and he'd tell or re-tell the old stories. I'd, in turn, offer up some memory that might rekindle one of his. And so we'd go.

Age-wise, Jim was 10 years younger than my father and just 12 years older than me. While he occupied a chronological mid-way point between father and son, it was remembering my dad, and all of the experiences they had shared working on the farm, that he would recollect with warmth and regard. As he linked me to that past, possibly I served a similar purpose.

Among my earliest memories was of Jim, squatted beside a cow during the evening milking and, when I wasn't looking, pointing the cow's teat in my direction and squirting me with milk. He'd tease my sister the same way.

He was there, among my rescuers after I got myself caught inside a steel-cylindered corn crib. The chute had plugged up with corn after I crawled through it and left me stranded. In retrospect, the matter was a minor one. However, my seemingly dangerous predicament had me scared.

I recall him getting mildly scolded by my father for taking the tractor down the lane to the back pasture to get the cows and, apparently being in a hurry, running them up to the barn, something you should never do with dairy cattle just before milking. I realize now that he might have had a date with Joyce later that night, so I understand the haste.

Jim worked as a hired man for other area farmers. He had a reputation for being an excellent dairy herdsman. He tried dairy farming on his own for a spell in the late '60s, operating a herd on the old Finlan

Farm in northern Conway Township. But, like other small-scale farmers, he eventually turned to a job with fewer hours and more dependable pay. He drove a semi truck for awhile and then went to work at the GM Proving Grounds in Milford. Still, he never lost nor gave up his affection for farm life.

Although Jim and I did a fair share of reminiscing, we would chat on other matters. It was his love for the seemingly mundane aspects of agriculture that stick out in my mind. During a conversation a couple of years ago, Jim told of how he was clearing brush on the Eggleston Farm, both to help out as well as to keep the place in shape. In return, he said, Doc Eggleston (a retired animal doctor) was teaching him how to handle and train the draft horses.

Jim had an apparent curiosity to try out different things like that. Not all of his "extracurricular activities" involved rural pastimes. For instance, he was among the fellows who helped Keith Liverance during funeral services. Underlying this motivation to "pitch in and help" was a curiosity about other people's experiences, and certainly an enjoyment of sharing their friendship. He once told me of visiting an elderly farmer who lived east of town and how it was important to learn about the old ways of doing different tasks before such knowledge was lost. Hearing that, I thought that the wrong person was working as a reporter in town. The sad irony is, having gained that knowledge for his own benefit (and presumably to pass onto a younger generation), we lost him way too soon.

Jim Campbell was about much more than what I've offered in this piece. My association with him, and what we shared, comprise only a small slice of his overall life. He was foremost a family man. Along with wife, he leaves four children, his mother and sisters, and other close relatives. He had many friends of his own generation, in addition to his older and younger pals.

I offer my remembrance as a way to pay tribute to a fellow who cared deeply about who and what we were; about the rhythms of the countryside, the daily and seasonal routines of farming, as well as the broader scope of agricultural activity. He was, as his wife said, "a farmer at heart" and that heart was good-sized. This caring attitude, shown in his words and deeds, served to remind me of my own farm roots, and of their importance.

But I also offer this testimonial for a purely selfish reason: to shed some tears for a departed friend, but a few tears, as well, for the now broken link… for all of those shared memories that Jim and I can no longer conjure up together.

On Progress

I'm sitting at a secluded picnic table on a wooded knoll that overlooks the lake. I've taken a walk from the nearby beach where the rest of the family is frolicking in the sand and swimming area. I pause here, in this isolated spot, shaded from the hot sun, and gaze out at the blue, partly cloudy sky and languid waters.

A serene setting, except in front of me are two jet skis, their young operators speeding them back and forth, then around in tight circles; the latter movement resembling a dog chasing its tail. If your criteria for advancement are noise, commotion, speed, and placing additional motorized floating craft upon our water wonderland, then jet skis are indeed an improvement to the human and natural conditions.

While I think it's good to have to paddle or row through some of life's waterways, I'm not adverse to the amenities of a trolling motor, the leisurely pontoon, or even the muffled hum of a motorboat. It's just that here, as in so many other areas and activities, we seem to roar right past the happy medium or the proper balance. Having done so, many apologists then defend the outcome as consumer choice (the consumer of noise given preference over the consumer of quiet) or, more often as another step in our progress.

During the Middle Ages, the king and his entourage often made tours through the realm, visiting the major cities along with stopping to see the area nobility. This was called a *royal progress*. The trips had assorted purposes, but collecting taxes was a main one. The lords and other officials of the kingdom, of course, gathered this wealth mainly from the farmers, herdsmen, and tradesmen who resided within the kingdom. In the best of situations, the aristocracy provided defense from marauders and a system of order and stability in exchange for these taxes. Frequently, though, the set-up was akin to a protection racket; a systematic plundering.

The word's meaning has spread out over the ensuing centuries, although it still possesses that economic connotation along with the idea of a physical journey. But the term, which can be used as either a noun or verb, also includes as its synonyms: advancement, development, and growth.

We've come to associate progress with moving towards a goal or ideal, or advancing towards maturity; or the completion of a task; and quite often as the gradual development of mankind and civilization. We tend to view progress, in this sense, as "a positive" or "an improvement." To our credit, many have questioned that concept, pointing out that while we're continuously changing, adapting, and rearranging— individually and overall— this movement does *not* automatically mean we're better off as a result. We've learned in retrospect that changes can bring unforeseen repercussions, trade-offs, losses, and ill effects.

Much change is beyond our control. When we make a decision or choose a course of action, there's often an ambiguity of consequences. Examining and wrestling with that, rather than blindly or unquestionably accepting the new alternative, to my mind shows we're making progress.

The questioning of whether change equals progress can be as personal as: "If I accept this job offer or marry this gal or guy, what'll happen?" to the broader-based: "How might computers influence or alter our culture for good or ill?" Certainly the matter of both individual and social progress covers a wide breadth. Still, as I noted, the definition (for many folks, if not most) remains strongly tied to economics and financial well-being —and whether we judge either or both to be improving or digressing. While economics may only be part of the larger tapestry of human endeavor, it's nevertheless a predominant part of the pattern. As such, on those occasions when we're discussing progress, we're often centering our focus on economic change and development and are inclined to view this as a social benefit regardless of any adverse fall out.

Locally, economic development has become a recurring term in our policy-making discussions and considerations. With residential growth picking up speed during the last several years, as was expected given the demographic trends of southeast Michigan, there has been a corresponding growth in commercial operations and activities, and a need for expanded services such as schools, law enforcement, ambulance, road maintenance, waste disposal, and sewer and water capacity.

As a community, we've attempted to plan for this anticipated growth through land-use plans and zoning ordinances, and to fashion a vision on how best to manage it. At the same time, to help offset the tax burdens and strained school and municipal budgets that this accelerating population causes, efforts have been made to bring industrial enterprises here.

The future is now, as they say. We're being economically developed. We're changing and being changed. The phenomenon seems new and sudden, yet it's not. This neck of the Michigan woods supported a hunting-and-gathering economy after the glaciers retreated some 10,000 years ago. Less than 200 years ago, with the arrival of American-European settlers, the area underwent the rapid transformation into an agricultural society. Coupled with that agrarian activity was the harvesting of natural resources, including fur-bearing wildlife, fish, lumber, iron ore, and copper.

The emergence of a manufacturing sector came soon after. The mass production of automobiles has dominated things for much of this century, although farming (as a way of life) held its own for a large segment of our population until the 1950s and 1960s.

All of that was change. Much of it fell within the category of economic development, with much of the development spurred by population shifts, technological innovations, and expanding human expectations. Whether all of this also constituted progress in the sense of advancement, improvement, and a positive outcome would be a topic worth pondering. Progress, as opposed to change, is often a human judgment. It's this judgment that needs to remain part of our current discussions and decision-making. As we begin to turn our cornfields into factories and stores, as more and more of our farmsteads become housing tracts, as our country roads evolve into busy thoroughfares, as our woodlots and overgrown meadows become golf courses and parks, the consideration of these various proposals ought always to include the possible negatives along with the benefits. The scope of discussion should not be limited to only economics. In managing this ongoing process of economic change, we should remember that the specter of the unforeseen consequence hovers amid the tangible pluses this growth might bring to the community.

In a free society, in a world that's constantly changing, we can't control all aspects. Nor should we wish to. But when we can and do make our decisions about a future course, it should include a weighing of possible repercussions as well as the tradeoffs. Any possible losses and ill effects should be added to the scales, balancing them with such important factors as an increased tax base, jobs creation, added goods and services, and upgrading infrastructure.

The values, ethics, and vision we bring to our deliberations will matter. They will be tested and opposed. In pushing for economic development, will we seek to soften any adverse impact to others? Will we reject certain proposals if the non-economic costs and those ill effects are judged as too high or too much? Or will those people (and whatever else lies in the way) be so much road kill? Where will our loyalty be? Will it be to friends and neighbors, to our customs and traditions, to our rural heritage, to the wild creatures and still-wild places, and to a sense of fairness and proportion? Or will our allegiance be to a different vision?

Change and innovation can mean progress, yet progress is not always an automatic consequence of change or the arrival of the latest technological gadget.

As I sit on the knoll beside the lake, enjoying this man-made environment of cleared underbrush, mowed lawns, nearby restrooms, and mosquito controls, but also savoring a secluded spot of the outdoors, I believe the only thing I could add to this example of human progress would be a permeating quietness, disturbed only by the sounds of wind, and of waves lapping against the shore. However, the jet skis share this moment and place, too. So I get up and make my progress back to the beach.

Winter: A Harsh Beauty

When winter showed up earlier this month, it was not like the silly fellow we'd been sparring with most of December, but rather the hard-eyed, hard-nosed, ruthless fellow that most of us recall from other past bouts. He landed a couple of hard jabs, just to let us know he was back and meant business, then he came across with a Joe Frazier-like left hook that sent us reeling. The temperatures dipped into the single digits, and the stiff breeze sent the wind-chill index well below zero. Now we know we're in for it… and can hunker down into our cold-weather mode until some faraway day in March when a balmy southern wind tells us that our ten-rounder with the Arctic Express is nearing the final bell.

As these things happen, the storm came on the day we drove over to Ithaca to attend a funeral and pay our respects to the Parcheta family. Fortunately, the roadway was fairly dry both going and coming back. There were frequent gusts that threatened a whiteout, mainly on the flat croplands north of St. Johns, still none proved long lasting.

On the return trip we stopped at a place called 'Ye Old Roadhouse' and found a table next to a tall, stone fireplace. A wood-burning insert set inside it, and the remnants of two or three logs still burned on this late afternoon.

The lunch special was beef stew which I ordered. When the waitress returned several minutes later, she brought a generous plate loaded with biscuits and a thick gravy of meat, potatoes, carrots and small onions. "Comfort food for a Michigan winter," I told my wife.

The stew and the extra warmth from the fire seemed just the right defense to bolster one against this first onslaught of frigid conditions.

Later, after we'd arrived home, son Bradley and I drove over to the boarding stable for his five o'clock riding lesson. The owner (and instructor) had called and left a message on the answering machine, wondering if we still planned to show up. "With the zero visibility, I thought you might not want to drive out," she said at the end of her message.

"Call her back, and tell her we'll be there," I told Bradley. Having just journeyed across a good portion of our fair state, I saw no reason to fear another four miles.

The country road leading to the farm had indeed drifted a bit. Despite those obstacles, my pick-up plowed splendidly through the accumulating snow. When we arrived, our horses were already in their stalls, chewing on their hay. The air inside the barn was cold; however, we were well-fortified in our long underwear, insulated overalls, sweatshirts, coats, hats, and gloves.

I got Bob out, while Bradley brought the tack from a nearby room. Saddled and bridled, the horse (with his rider astride) soon appeared in the adjacent arena. The instructor, who with her husband had been busy feeding the other horses in another barn, came in. She was dressed in a heavy coat, leggings, and earmuffs, so all of us were ready for business.

After watching the lesson for awhile, and moving around to stay warm, I decided to go outside and enjoy the storm. A blizzard can wreak havoc on our suburban culture, making a rush-hour commute or a motor trip on a crowded freeway both nerve wracking and potentially dangerous. Getting stranded, being away from the safety of a warm shelter, is a major fear most of us have. Still, there is something fascinating about such foul weather. It gives a hint of menace and danger. The snow-covered landscape on this early evening, shadowy in the dim light, appeared both foreboding and mysterious. The trees, black and gnarled, had an eerie look as they stood silhouetted against the darkening backdrop. The overcast sky, veiled by the blowing snow, possessed a harsh beauty, like an evil seductress tempting us towards our doom.

My path took me alongside the barn, marring the smooth surface, then I headed up a knoll to the paddocks. A few of the horses were kept outside. Most had sought the protection of the lean-to shelters, safe from the wind and wind-driven snowfall. But a few remained outside, still eating hay. From this modest height, I could see the surrounding pastures, the thin lines of the fences, the lighted arena and nearby house, and the other outbuildings.

Our annual bout with winter is often hard, difficult, and challenging. It can test one's will and fortitude. Those left hooks can leave one staggered and discouraged. But these hard elements also awaken and refresh the senses. For those who roam these dark Michigan hillsides, they are the stuff of life and living.

On a Trail Ride

We rode the horses up a steep hill, using a path worn from much use. At one spot a small gully had formed, the top soil washed away from the lack of ground cover. We guided the horses alongside it, careful to avoid any misstep.

An overgrown meadow, dry and brittle looking from the lack of any recent rain, flanked each side of our trail. Halfway to the peak stood a lonely tree, its foliage spare and mangy, offering little shade were a weary wanderer to seek relief under the branches.

But on this mild day we needed no such relief. The sky overhead on this Sunday afternoon stretched clear and blue with only wisps of clouds. September had thus far been kind, extending out the line of summer days much longer than one could reasonably hope. Even though we know our northern weather can turn on a dime with the inevitable cold front producing in its wake gray, rainy and overcast skies, we secretly harbor the illusion that these soothing days might linger on and on, perhaps going on without end.

Earlier in the morning, knowing what ultimately lay ahead in the long-range autumn forecast, I had taken a look outside, and suggested to my son— who was camped out on the living room recliner, watching cartoons— that we go on a trail ride.

"We won't get too many more days like this one," I pointed out.

Bradley, though, didn't need any convincing. A couple of hours later we had driven out to the boarding stable, saddled the unsuspecting horses, and were now starting the first leg of the ride. I led the way atop Huck, our seven-year-old sorrel quarter horse who possesses a bold outlook on life, Bradley followed on Bob, an older, dapple-gray gelding whose temperament is the opposite; he's skittish about unexpected noises and unfamiliar sights and is a great believer in the wisdom of a hasty retreat.

The owners of the stable have created several pathways on their 168-acre farm for this sort of adventure. These paths circle around the different crop fields and pastures as well as the perimeter of the farm. They also crisscross, giving a rider different options. They've also made them user-friendly by running a brush hog over the route, keeping the weeds from growing too high.

The farm, like the surrounding countryside, is hilly, but once you reach the crest of this rise, the land levels off towards the west, with only one small dip, until it reaches the far road. On this flatter piece of ground the owners have planted a field of soybeans on the right side of the trail, and a stand of corn to the left. Beyond the corn, southward, is a small woodlot, while bordering the bean field to the north is a combination of trees and uncultivated grassland. If you chose to head north rather than west, the trail goes down into a ravine, and then climbs back up to an alfalfa field.

Well aware of Bob's nervousness, I steer Huck into the path between the corn and soybeans. While the route that goes beside the woods is more scenic, a number of deer reside on the farm, and I'm not anxious to have one bolt unexpectedly near us, causing the horses, namely Bob, to lurch in alarm and turn tail at a wild gallop.

This behavior is a survival instinct for this grazing animal that over many thousands of years has evolved quick reflexes and speed to avoid or outrun assorted predators. However, this reflex is apt to leave a rider on the ground.

On the other hand, the sound of moving horses and creaking saddles, along with our scent, should adequately warn the nearby bucks and does to skedaddle. I hedge my bets by periodically singing, "Deerie, Deerie, Deerie." As I sing, I imagine myself as a long-ago cowboy, crooning a song at night to reassure the resting longhorns.

"Why are you singing like that?" my son asks the first time I croon.

"To scare off the deer," I reply. And pause.

There's no comeback. Bradley, unlike his father, is not yet a wise guy and does not think to retort, "That'll do the trick."

The owners call their place *Everview*. Up here on the high plateau, it's plain to understand why. All around us, from every vantage point, you can visually feast on a horizon of long green ridges simmering in the bright sunlight.

Huck moves confidently along the trail as I sing away the deer and any other creatures within earshot. Bob follows behind. The lack of moisture has dried out the crops. The beans are already a harvest brown, while the leaves on the corn stalks have begun to whither and droop, needing only a killer frost to finish off the job.

At the end of the fields are two houses, and just beyond is a graveled road. These parcels, I assume, were once part of the farm, but had been sold off by a previous owner. The appearance of these buildings would seem benign, yet Huck, as we near them, becomes unsure of the situation. Caution takes hold, and he stops and glances back at the route behind us. I suspect he's telling himself that we've had enough adventure for one day, and that the prudent choice would be to turn around, retrace our steps, and go home. "Who knows what lies ahead?" he's probably thinking or "What dangers might these dwellings pose?"

I do not share his concerns, although he may well be the wiser one. I kick his sides, tap his rump with the reins, and finally coax him forward.

Once past these human habitats, Huck resumes his assured manner. We ride along the width of the corn field and then circle back, the path now taking us between the corn and the woods. With the prolific whitetails more likely to be in this area, I start singing again.

Several hunting blinds have been constructed around the acreage, with most of them situated at intervals along the edge of this small forest. They are strategically placed sites that offer an unobstructed shot at any deer crossing the soon-to-be open span of corn stubble as well as good views of the small clearings in the woods. I imagine the farm is a lively place every November 15th when the firearm deer season opens.

Huck and Bob are wary as we approach these makeshift shelters; however, having survived the houses, they are less nervous, and do not stop. As we move down a small slope and up the ensuing rise, I can see a couple of does grazing on the trail up ahead. I quickly yell out "Deer," alerting Bradley. They spot us at the same instance and are already vanishing into the cover of the brush. Shortly afterwards, I catch sight of several wild turkeys feeding next to the corn. Almost at the same moment they notice our approach, and fly off. "So far so good," I think.

That optimism proves short-lived. As my son questions me about the differences between these wild turkeys and the domesticated variety we feast on each Thanksgiving, a deer suddenly crashes out of the corn just ahead of us. Huck starts to run forward, but I'm able to pull his neck to the right with the rein and bring him to a stop, just as I'd mentally rehearsed doing. Bob, meanwhile, as we've learned to expect, did a quick reverse pivot— a maneuver he seems unwilling to perform in front of a judge during a showmanship pattern— and takes off like Abbott & Costello fleeing from Frankenstein. Bradley, having become a good rider, stays in the saddle and stops him within a short distance.

"Well, that was fun," I comment.

These unexpected moments, fraught with the possibility of injury, are among the risks you take when mounted on a horse. The scenario is similar to what a farrier once told me about his trade, "When you shoe horses it's not *if* you'll be kicked, but only a matter of *when.*" Having been kicked by a few cows in my youth, and chased a couple of times by bulls, I have a healthy respect for large animals no matter how tame acting any of them might seem.

Still, I'm not fatalistic. I have no willingness to accept the inevitability of *when*, any more than I figure it's only a matter of time before I crash my pickup into a tree. I hope that prudence, caution, and lots of practice in the saddle will be effective antidotes to taking a spill, or otherwise getting hurt. Nevertheless, the peril is always present. If it's not deer spooking your horse, it could be a ground nest of hornets getting riled up, their repeated stings causing your otherwise trusty steed to rear and buck, or else an unseen burrow that trips your animal, sending you up and over its head.

The trail soon takes us away from the woods, then back through the overgrown meadow— the flowers and plants having decorated the landscape with their autumn blooms as well as their burrs and ripening seeds. Then we go down into the ravine. I lean back, standing up a bit in the stirrups to assist Huck, helping him keep his balance as he carefully descends step by step.

Once at the bottom we ride back up the incline, the two horses trotting to gain momentum, and reach the alfalfa field. As with the corn and beans, a trail has been groomed alongside the edges and we follow it. Here, in a more open space, the horses seem to relax. The only critters we stir up now are the various birds. We begin to circle the field, walking next to a tree line and an old rusting wire mesh fence, parts of it gone. The trees and fence separate this farm from the neighboring homestead.

The second cutting of hay had been mowed and baled earlier in the month. Enough re-growth has occurred since then to make this stretch of ground resemble a large, inviting lawn. A hay field in my youth meant work, part of a routine of daily toil that I did not always find enjoyable. But now, with the warm sun overhead and the smell of the perspiring horse, the scene and moment are pleasant enough, those youthful rigors having become the stuff of pleasant remembrance and wistful tales. Still, there's a tinge of the bittersweet to the setting. Like an impending sad good by or a regretful farewell, the pleasure of the experience is clouded by an awareness of what lies ahead… and what has been, or soon will be, lost. The turning of another season, a changing landscape where agriculture is gradually giving way to sprawl; a rural way of life that long ago disappeared from my life, and has been gradually receding from much of the Michigan countryside. Gone also are many of those family, friends, and neighbors who once shared this time and place. Yet loss and change are among the relentless readjustments that accompany the advancing years. We deal with it, and move on.

The teenager riding behind me, with all the promises of the future, gazes steadily forward. I also study the trail ahead, ready to employ whatever wits and wiles I possess to meet unexpected circumstances; still, I'm guilty of looking back more and more at the path that's been covered.

As we near the stable and the end of our afternoon outing, there remains one more ravine to go down, and back up. My legs and lower back have begun to ache. Unlike Bradley, who rides on a more regular basis, I'm not accustomed to the rigors of hard leather and a moving horse. I believe I'll need a hot shower when we're home.

Huck is again hesitant; the slope here is steeper than the others. I understand his reluctance, but decide we're bound to try, and see what happens. Others have followed this by-way and survived without mishap. So might we. With a little nudge from me, he goes forward. Bob, the willing follower, is several yards behind.

We make it down. And back up. No sweat. Soon we're in sight of the other horses grazing in the paddocks, and finally the house and barns. Sore muscles (I decide) are a small price to pay for scenic vistas, for a chance to re-visit these transitory places where cultivation blends into untamed nature; where livestock and herdsmen still share the land with turkey and deer.

Despite the aches and concerns, we push on, take our chances, and accept the risks. While there are no guarantees, we anticipate some reward for the effort. Soon enough the cold winds will blow, and all too soon the years will recede. All too soon, there'll be no more balmy afternoons to ride a horse… or share the trail with this (still) young rider.

On This Cool Autumn Morning

On this cool autumn morning I watch a hawk gliding in effortless sweeps above the neighbor's overgrown meadow. I notice as well a trio of our cats wandering about the hayfield next to the barn. The local predators are busy, it seems.

With pen in hand I'm also attempting to put some food on the table, albeit by a more convoluted means than the circling hawk or the prowling kitty cats. A number of middlemen and financial transactions lie between my current toil and the resulting nourishment. I'm not totally removed from the food chain though. Our freezer is filled with packages of meat from one of the steers we purchased as a calf, fed daily, and— once he became as plump as a holiday turkey— hauled off to the butcher. Yet even here a layer or two insulate me from my prey, with the butcher doing the hard work.

That was not the case a couple of generations before. My Grandpa Lloyd would regale us with the glories of his days as a young farmer. Among his anecdotes was the tale of how he'd dip a hog (presumably dead by then) into a boiling barrel of water, scald it, and then scrape off the bristles. I could only imagine this scene since by then he'd quit raising swine, focusing instead on dairy cattle and raising crops, and (I assume) having no desire to re-live that bygone chore. The smell of the scalded hog and the task of removing those bristles, I'm sure, had their down side.

I remember telling my mother, a number of years ago, that I was writing a story— one of my many abortive efforts to create short fiction— which opened with the old farmer slaughtering several of his chickens.

"The wind suddenly picked up, blowing in from the northwest," it began. "It rattled the dry, dead corn stalks and stirred up the smoldering fire under the iron kettle, sending the smoke swirling about. Sitting next to the kettle, filled with hot water, Billy Durfee looked up from his work. The morning was cool. The frost had earlier coated the lawn with a white sheen, but the heat from the fire kept Billy warm as he plucked the feathers from the dead chickens."

The problem, I told my mother, was that I needed to find out exactly how to prepare the chickens and, afterwards, how to can them. I had a pretty good idea that the chickens, having lost their heads on the chopping block, would be gutted and hung upside down on a line of wire or twine to drain off the remaining blood, then dipped (like my grandfather's hog) into boiling water. With the feathers loosened,

Billy Durfee would pull them off, including the removal of those pesky pinfeathers.

I had only a vague notion about the rest of the process. I knew I could have my protagonist (who by the way is a bachelor) stick the cleaned poultry into a freezer and be done with that part of the story. But I figured a farmer of that generation, growing up in the early years of the 20th century before electricity had reached this rural hinterland, and before electric freezers became commonplace, someone still practicing the old arts of agriculture, might prefer to continue canning his chicken.

To my surprise Mom knew all about this activity. “Your Grandma Amo used to raise chickens,” she told me. “We’d can them every year.”

Mother, who seldom shared fond memories about the chores of her youth, usually the opposite, and who couldn’t get off the farm fast enough after my father died, had an excited tone to her voice as she provided me the details.

“The chicken broth made fabulous gravy,” she noted. “We’d fix chicken and dumplings.”

“It was hard to keep your weight down with that gravy,” she added as a practical aside. At my request, she wrote down the specifics, the step-by-step recipe that Billy Durfee would have followed when canning his chickens.

My story never got past that opening passage. I failed to dream up anything too dramatic or interesting for old Billy to do that day after he cleaned his birds. I envisioned him as a humorous fellow, with a quick wit. The humor and wit would come to the forefront when he interacted with others; it would permeate his conversation. By himself, however, he would convey a darker, more somber inner monologue. Billy would also be a counterbalance to his older brother John, a family man with children and young grandchildren (including my alter ego Phillip). John practiced an “all work, no play” view of farming. Only Billy, with his jokes and amusing comments, with his sometimes outlandish remarks and observations, could crack the usually stern demeanor of his brother. As for Phillip, his Uncle Billy was both a source of information and a pal.

I’d grown up around men like Billy and John, most of them a mix of hard work and amused outlook. The intent of my story was to convey their unique and vibrant personalities, and to offer as best I could, a glimpse of this way-of-life… the arts of agriculture they practiced on a daily and seasonal basis. I figured on a cool autumn morning that one of them, Billy, might be sitting next to a kettle of hot water, busy with this chore, yet hearing the dry leaves rattling in the wind, knowing that the task of harvesting the corn awaited him. However, in between those jobs he might head into town for a game of cards or drive over to see what his hard-working brother might be up to.

And, while picking off those feathers, he might notice a hawk circling about, or a trio of cats on the prowl, and remember his grandfather and mother, both of them now departed; one who used to tell of scalded hogs, and the other of rich chicken gravy.

The End of a 4-H Career

And just like that it's over.

On a hot, humid Saturday we took part in the State 4-H Horse Show, held each August at Michigan State University. On the following afternoon we joined our 4-H club, Bridles & Bits, at the Yankee Springs Horsemen's Campground for the annual potluck meal, followed by the kick-off meeting that launches a new year for members.

For our son, however, who is heading towards his 19th birthday and his freshman classes at Grand Valley State University, the show and the meeting marked the end of his 4-H career. We joined the organization when he was 11. I say "we" (his mother and I being part of that plural pronoun) since parents seem as much participants as the kids— although at times some of them are more involved than maybe they should be.

The State Show brings many of the best young riders and horses from around Michigan to this venue. We've been fortunate to have qualified in previous years, so the hustle and bustle— which at first glance might seem a chaotic mess— was familiar. We knew where to go, and what to do; a far cry from our first trip here.

Bradley, with his quarter horse Keno, had been taking *dressage* lessons for the past year, aiming his future at that challenging riding discipline. During the fair and in other 4-H competitions, he'd also competed in the English hunt seat classes and done well; but for the State Show it was an either-or choice. Since he'd invested a lot of time and effort in *dressage*, and even though he is still very much a beginner in this riding technique, he decided to sign up for those events.

We had always attended State Show with hopes of success. In the past Bradley had earned a couple of placement ribbons. But he'd never finished first or second, receiving one of those coveted blue or red ribbons, and also qualifying to move onto the Grand Championship round.

He and *Keno* did not fare well in their final 4-H outing. Riding competition— unlike the speed classes or horse racing— are subjective affairs. The judge, hired on that particular day by organizers, rules the roost. This person's likes and dislikes, interpretations, observations, and inclinations are part of the evaluation. True, there's a set of established criteria to go by; still, the word 'judge' inherently implies just that. As a veteran 4-H leader once counseled me when we were discussing (I in an exasperated tone) the vagaries of these lords of the horse ring, namely how one judge's placements can be so different from another's…"All you're doing is paying a person for an opinion."

Cream generally rises to the top. Good riders and horses, for the most part, place well from one judge to the next. Nevertheless, there have been a few shows where Bradley and his mount seemed to "walk on water." The blue ribbons flowed towards him like a high tide. Of course, we thought that this judge was "just dandy." There have been other occasions where, if you took it to heart, you'd come away thinking the horse should be sold to the glue factory, and the boy should try his hand at exhibiting goats.

On this final outing the judge did not score our entry with much favor. It was an admittedly disappointing way to finish the 4-H years. No happy, storybook ending occurred for our high hopes. However, we've had our share of successes. So, we move onto a new day, and the next adventure.

But 4-H is not all about competitions and ribbons. There has been all of the fun that the kids (and even adults) have had at the fair as well as the campouts, trail rides, sledding parties, roller skating trips, and the monthly club meetings. More importantly has been the camaraderie among the youngsters who've grown up together, and the friendships we've made with other families. At the potluck meeting on Sunday afternoon, Bradley and two fellow 4-H retirees— Tasha and Leah— were called up by the leader, and given going-away gifts. The leader, Cheryl, provided a brief anecdote about each of them.

"When Brad joined the club he was only about this tall," she said, placing her hand much closer to the ground than our six-foot two-inch son now stands. "And he was very quiet and very shy. I think we got him over that."

She then offered comments about the two young ladies, kidding that neither of them suffered from shyness, and concluded her remarks by telling them, "We'll miss the three of you, and we wish each of you the best as you head to college."

Eight years have come and gone. A boy I once had to help get up on the saddle has grown into an accomplished young man. The eyes get misty despite one's stoic attempt to stifle the emotion. 4-H has been a great ride. And just like that it's over.

Graduation Day: A Time of Hopes and Dreams

This coming Sunday, barring an unforeseen mishap, I'll again be kneeling at the side of an aisle, camera in hand, waiting for the opening notes of "Pomp and Circumstance." Then in pairs or as threesomes, the soon-to-be graduates of the Class of 2010 at Fowlerville High will begin walking from the back entrance of the gym to their seats in front. Assembled there to observe them (besides yours truly) and to share this landmark occasion will be parents, siblings, grandparents, and special friends.

The graduating classes in recent years have ranged around 200 students— smaller than our neighboring schools in Howell and Pinckney— but large enough in number that it takes awhile for each member to stroll briskly past me. I haven't room in the newspaper for photographs of all these deserving students, so the pictures I take are spur-of-the-moment decisions.

There are several, though— usually athletes that I've taken pictures of with their sports teams during the past four years— whose faces have become familiar. Several of these seniors, and any others I might recognize, will most likely find themselves in next week's paper. The other images I select are done solely by chance, the main criteria being how well the picture turned out.

In addition, I plan to take photographs of the class president, the valedictorian, and salutatorian as well as this year's guest speaker. I always do so at the start of the respective addresses so as not to distract either the speaker or the audience once the address has gotten underway. Once this journalistic duty is accomplished, I take a seat off to the side and listen to what each has to offer.

Like the board of education members who sit in a row along the back of the *dais*, donned in black robes (a rough outfit to wear when it's warm and muggy), I've heard my share of speeches. The guest orators, usually a favorite teacher or class sponsor, have on the whole been entertaining as well as reflective. They have been advised to keep the talk reasonably short. And most do. A handful of them, the naturals who are able to mix a heartfelt message with a good seasoning of humor, have finished to an enthusiastic and grateful applause.

The assorted valedictorians, salutatorians, and class presidents have been a mixed bag. The presidents, as a rule, get to be presidents because they're extroverted and confident. Those traits carry over in the presentation of their talks. The top two academic students (some years there are more than two) might also possess those speech-giving characteristics, or they may be nervous, meek of voice, and read the text with head down. No matter. They've earned the right to be up at the podium. This is their special day, and I try to listen in a respectful and attentive manner. God knows, I didn't come even close to earning that honor back when I attended the hallowed halls of Fowlerville High. My respectable 'B' average got me a seat at the ceremony and a chance to continue my education at Michigan State University, but not any invitation to offer my counsel at our graduation.

On June 12, 1969, on a hot, sweltering Thursday night inside the gym of what's now Munn Middle School, Paul Grill, our class president, gave the Welcome Address, while two of our Top 10 classmates, Connie Tomlin and Jim Walker, provided the Student Addresses. For the record, Sherry Maleitzke was the Valedictorian. The tradition back then was for the girl to ask a boy to escort her as they walked down the aisle. My good friend Patty Roche did me the honor.

The main thing I remember about the evening, other than the humidity, was that a group of us sang the "Impossible Dream" midway through the ceremony. This title song from the Broadway play *Man of La Mancha* (i.e. Don Quixote) was then (and still should be) a graduation standard.

Actually I did not sing. At least not very loud. I had been invited to participate in this chorus, but the teacher overseeing our rehearsals, and who accompanied us on piano, quickly discovered that I sang in rather flat notes, a bit off key, and that my somewhat deep voice stuck out. After a few futile attempts to improve my delivery, she politely asked if I'd be so kind as to mouth the words. Our vocal music teacher in elementary school, Mr. James Wong, had made a similar request of me years before, so I was prepared. This flat singing voice has proven a cruel fate, since my innermost desire has been to be a crooner, moving the audience with a stirring and lyrical voice, rather than dabbling (as I've done these many years) in journalistic lingo.

On that night, softly, ever so softly, I sang with the rest of the performers the lyrics of that familiar song. They seemed to speak to my own aspirations; metaphors of youthful longing. An impossible dream. An unreachable star. Following the quest.

There'll be a few students who'll sing at the Sunday commencement. No doubt they've been blessed with voices that are both stirring and lyrical. Their inspiring song, the band performing a final piece with its senior musicians, along with the speeches and the presentation of the long-awaited diploma are all part of the pomp and circumstance. I can't think of a better way to spend a couple of hours than witnessing this traditional rite of passage.

The cliché, one you're bound to hear at least once at each ceremony, is that this is not just the end of a student's journey through school, but the start of a new destination. The poignancy is that, as a class, they'll never be assembled altogether again "as one"... just as my gang of '69-ers never was. We depart, forever ending our shared association, and head off to our respective new lives.

You look out each June at the young, eager faces and think about your own journey from that long ago Commencement Night to where you are now. Others in the audience, I'm sure, are doing the same. There are dreams and hopes aplenty at graduation, they permeate the air. Some of them may be impossible and unreachable, others more practical and obtainable, but dreams nevertheless; dreams of hope and aspiration. When you start a new journey, as these graduates will this Sunday, I think a dream is a good thing to take along.

Deer Hunting

Two of my grandsons, Andrew and Josh, are in the woods at the back end of our farm, their bows and arrows at ready, hoping to bag a deer. I hear a light rain hitting against the window, so I realize (as feared when we heard the weather forecast last night) that they are not enjoying optimal conditions as they sit in their tree stands on this first day of the archery season.

I had gone out the weekend before with the youngest one, Josh, chaperoning him during Michigan's youth hunt. It was about six o'clock in the morning when we trudged from the house to his makeshift deer blind, he carrying a single-shot 20 gauge gun and I had a pair of backless folding stools. The weather that morning was near perfect. The stars in the final hour of darkness were vibrant, and I noticed the handle of the Big Dipper was pointed earthward. After reaching our hunting spot, we watched (and waited) as the false dawn gradually lightened the countryside and veiled the glittering sky.

The blind Josh had erected was situated among the trees on the property line and overlooked the area of the hayfield that borders a small swale and overgrown wood lot. The quiet on that morning, as they say, was deafening. We could hear the occasional car driving by, loud and distinct despite being a half-mile away as well as the neighbor's barking dog. The pre-dawn was so still and listless that I stifled the urge to cough or clear my throat, fearing the noise, being out-of-place here, would scare off any nearby deer.

Patience and fortitude are what it often takes to be successful. Unlike the opening hours of the firearms season when the surrounding forests and fields are invaded by dozens of hunters, sending the bucks scurrying about in alarm, nothing much was happening on this morning to "get them moving." Our hope rested on the possibility that at some point during the morning one or two deer, preferably a buck with a nice set of antlers, would saunter out of the cover to graze on the hay or decide to choose this clearing to migrate from one locale to another. There are countless other places, either here on the farm and elsewhere, that the deer can graze or travel across, so our prospects at this spot, while appearing good, were still a matter of chance.

Back in my younger years there'd often be a half-dozen or more of us— cousins and friends— in our Saturday hunting parties. Our preferred method of trying to bag deer, at least the one preferred by the older cousins who were in charge, was to drive a section. My mock complaint, then and now, was that as a junior member of the firm, I generally got to drive on those days when it was warm. Since I was usually overdressed and had no place to discard the extra clothing, I would become hot and sweaty as I worked my way through the thick and thorny undergrowth. But on the frostier afternoons, when exercise was just what the doctor ordered to stay warm, I instead got drafted to stand. I remember, without much fondness, how the chill air would pierce through my too light of a coat and numb my fingertips.

In either case, whether doing sentry duty, or 'on the move,' I never made a successful shot. In fact, I rarely even saw the quarry we were after. When our group did land a buck, it always seemed to be one of the older cousins or one of their friends that enjoyed the honors, regardless of whether they happened to be driving the deer that day or standing.

I did have one "can't miss" opportunity, but came away empty handed. (And with no regrets.) We were driving an overgrown meadow, with lots of brush. As I walked through the tall grasses and brush, I suddenly saw the buck standing a short distance from me. He stood silhouetted against a clump of poplar saplings, maybe 40 yards in front of me and a little to my left. Luck, I thought, had finally come my way… still I hesitated. Being on a drive, I had a cousin also to my left. I had lost track of him in the thick cover. Unable to see or hear him, I couldn't be sure if he was trailing in back of me, was parallel, or might even be ahead of me (possibly behind the deer.)

I listened and looked. And within a moment the buck, having decided I meant trouble, bounded off. I yelled, "Deer coming!" in hopes one of those standing up ahead would hear and be alerted, but as I recall no shots were fired.

These days the deer are more plentiful. That increase in numbers, along with the sale of doe permits, has greatly increased the possibility of a gratifying outcome. Both grandsons bagged a deer last year. Perhaps that memory— the lingering taste of accomplishment— will reinforce their patience and fortitude as they sit in their respective tree stands on this wet and miserable morning. Perhaps it will help dispel any regret they may feel about leaving their warm, dry beds and will keep them scanning the woods for a glimpse of tawny brown, that telltale sign of a cautiously approaching whitetail.

The Harsh Word

The horses always seem pleased when I appear in the morning. They begin moving about their stalls, a couple of them stomping their hooves, and there is much whinnying. The psychological term for this is 'conditioned reflex'. They see me, and get excited. But there is an underlying reason. If you'll recall, the Russian physiologist, Ivan Petrovich Pavlov, conducted studies on dogs, ringing a bell with the appearance of food. Eventually the animals came to associate the noise with this meal, and would salivate at the sound, even on those occasions when no food appeared. These exercises on conditioned reflexes are called "the foundation of behavioral psychology."

So it is not I, but rather the sweet feed that I supply them soon after arriving in the barn that stirs their fondness.

A couple of the horses also urinate in their stalls shortly after my entrance, apparently having held it as long as possible. This makes cleaning up after them a bit messier than it would be otherwise; however, I have no idea how to persuade these noble steeds to wait until I've taken them outside to their paddock.

The Hereford calves have also come to think of me as their personal chef. They begin mooing at the sight of me, continuing their pleas until I've put a bucket of grain into their trough. I don't generally feed the barn cats, leaving that task to my wife, so they don't express as much enthusiasm at my morning appearance.

I haven't studied enough psychology to offer any detailed insights into conditioned reflexes. I can speculate that there are many things we, as humans, do and think that is the result of such subliminal cause and effect. "What makes a person tick?" can be difficult to fathom because we are unaware of which stimulus, ingrained at an early age, triggers a specific behavior or reaction. That reaction or behavior might be laudable; thus, the cause serves a beneficial purpose. But the response might be less exemplary, which is usually what captures our attention and causes us to speculate.

One of the conditionings of youth, meant to inspire proper or acceptable behavior, is punishment. "Spare the rod and spoil the boy" used to be the Golden Rule of child rearing. And "yes" there were those school masters who "taught to the tune of a hickory stick."

Much of what was considered as good parenting, back in the good old days, is now, in society's eyes, viewed as bordering on child abuse. Even spanking, once as common as the cold, is not considered by many as a proper response to a child's inappropriate behavior.

We've all witnessed that seemingly spoiled youngster, acting up in public, who in the dark recesses of our thoughts we'd like to take over our knee and "tan the kid's hide." Also, we've all seen a parent who puts on a display of overbearing authority; a meanness that makes you cringe in sympathy for the young, helpless victim.

In general, I've never been too impressed with the practice or advocacy of spanking, or otherwise striking a kid at every provocation or miscue; even less so when the intent is to deliberately inflict pain, or is done in front of others, causing humiliation. My impression is that this parental behavior does not inspire nor appeal to a child's better nature, but rather creates fear. Underlying that fear is a resentment or grievance at having been wronged. The child might indeed behave better: just like a whipped dog does, cringing in submission, careful and wary so as not to provoke another outburst.

Secondly, as we've been told by those professionals who deal with family abuse, this practice becomes hard-wired into the brain as the role model for child rearing. The child grows up, has his or her own sons and daughters, and, alas, the acorn does not fall too far from the oak tree. Similar techniques of physical punishment (or abuse) are employed.

The harsh word or humiliating taunt is often used as a substitute in the parental arsenal. While the father or mother may not actually strike the child, the words can leave a welt as painful as any caused by a leather belt. But these wounds are not as easily detectible or as easily combated. A school employee or the staff in the emergency room notices the telltale signs of physical abuse; and, as required by law, alerts the police. The cruelty of the tongue and the harm it can inflict, however, are less evident.

We live in a world where anger, frustration, substance abuse, and assorted resentments can result in all sorts of bad behavior by adults, especially towards children. An unnecessarily hard punishment, when inflicted on their children, unfortunately is a convenient outlet.

Many point to the child or teenager who is acting up or getting in trouble as deserving or needing punishment. And in some fashion, they do. But the undisciplined, over-reacting parent— the other half of this social equation— oftentimes needs to be considered when judging the situation. The actions of an adult (in a parental role) can be as much the cause of the problem as is the child's behavior. The notion that we are handcuffing parents and school officials by not allowing them free use of the rod or hickory stick or that it's OK for them to constantly berate a youngster is wrong.

I make this claim knowing full well, both as a parent and grandparent, that none of us are perfect. Even with the best of intentions, too often we make mistakes and missteps, letting our anger and frustration slip past their internal boundaries. We are not always careful or prudent with our words. However, this is something to be regretted and improved upon, rather than excused or rationalized. In the end you have to be a parent, not a buddy; yet neither should you be a tormentor. The parental role requires a measure of self-awareness, self-control and measured responses. We learn.

The harsh words sting and can be painful. Over time, if repeated often enough, they cause mental and emotional wounds that linger. Those wounds may eventually heal— but they leave scars. While these scars may now be old, still they remain. They're mingled there, in memory, with the bonds of affection; no longer as painful or raw, but never quite healed or forgotten.

Despite my vanity, I know it is not my smiling face that prompts excitement from the horses and calves when I show up each morning. Rather, it's the gratifying food: an understandable reflex, conditioned by experience. The reflex and response of our children and grandchildren, when we appear, is the result of a different sort of nourishment. I hope it is the words and acts of encouragement, and of my affection, that they will remember; that have helped to inspire them. The further hope is that my efforts at parental guidance and punishment are seen as fair and appropriate, and will serve as a good model when they eventually deal with their own children and grandchildren. As for those imprudent words that I have uttered, I hope they understand that these were slips of the tongue, and not of the heart. A scar is not a legacy I wish to pass on.

Mackinac Bridge: Connecting Michigan

The five miles of steel and concrete that span the Straits of Mackinac, connecting Michigan's two peninsulas, long ago became a combination landmark, tourist attraction, and icon. The elegant outline with the two main towers and the curved steel cables is easily recognizable to anyone who's previously viewed it, or seen a picture.

I remarked to my son Bradley as we stood on the Lake Huron side of the bridge, a few feet from the stone-littered shoreline with the sound of traffic rumbling overhead, that these towers and the lacework of cables are what make the difference.

"If it was just a long bridge with a railing, no one would find it that attractive," I explained. He agreed.

The Mackinac Bridge opened for use on Nov. 1, 1957 and the following June, during the bridge's dedication ceremony, the public was offered the opportunity to walk across the span. Sixty-eight of those who attended the event, including then Governor G. Mennen 'Soapy' Williams, availed themselves of this opportunity, going from Mackinaw City to St. Ignace. The walk was changed to Labor Day in 1959, but did not draw large participation during the first few years. In 1964 the direction was changed, with the start being in the Upper Peninsula. Could anyone have imagined back then, 54 years ago, how this tradition would grow and evolve?

Earlier this month over 36,000 walkers made the trek on a cool and windy morning with a threat of rain in the forecast. The number was down from the 42,000 of the previous year, and a far cry from the record 85,000 who joined President George H. Bush and Gov. John Engler in 1992. Even so, that's a lot of people.

The disc jockey at the live radio remote, standing on a makeshift platform at the entrance of the bridge, called out "Who's a first timer?" I, along with a number of others around me, raised our hands.

"Where you from?" he also called out. As I passed by him, I yelled, "Fowlerville!"

That's not my legal residence, but having grown up and worked here in the 'Palm of the Mitten' for most of the past 60 years, that's where I'm from.

Bradley was making his second trip on foot across the Mighty Mac, while my wife Dawn, who'd done it a few times before she hooked up with me, figured this was her sixth Labor Day Walk. Earlier, waiting in Mackinaw City for the bus that would take us across, we chatted with a family. The parents indicated that they'd been taking part for nearly 20 years.

"What's the lure?" I wondered as I stood in the motel parking lot, the morning still dark, careful not to drink too much coffee since I'd only get one chance to use a restroom before beginning the long hike.

A group of ambitious joggers were already underway by the time our bus reached the St. Ignace toll booth. The year before Governor Jennifer Granholm had joined that group. A number of people on the bus wondered if the new governor, Rick Snyder, was present. As it turned out, he had shown up, and— according to the news story I read the next day— he maintained "a brisk walking pace" and "finished the five miles in a little over an hour."

Brisk pace was what I aimed for, but surrounded by dozens of people and with a few thousand already crowded ahead of us, "slow and steady" turned out to be a more accurate description. Only one half of the bridge, the two northbound lanes, is open for pedestrians. The cars and trucks, using the other half, whizzed by us as they traveled in both directions. Midway across, at that section of the structure that's suspended, the wind caused the bridge to sway (as it's designed to do), causing all of us to become unsteady in our forward progress. Feeling a bit out of sync by the motion, I said to my family, "I can see why people get seasick on a rocking boat."

National Guard soldiers were stationed every few yards, standing either at the railing or on the traffic divide. Below, on the wavy waters, a pair of Sheriff marine patrol boats cruised back and forth. The memory of 9-11, only a few days away from its 10th anniversary, made the terrorist threat plausible. But crowd control and discouraging any foolhardy behavior, particularly near the railing, seemed more apparent priorities.

I enjoyed the scenery and the up-close look at the bridge. The height— 199 feet at midspan— did not bother me nor did the sight of the water far below when I glanced down through the steel grating that comprises a stretch of the road's surface. The grating, I later learned, is used to reduce the wind resistance.

The variety and multitude of my fellow walkers were what most impressed me. They came from all over Michigan as well as neighboring states. Young and old, and all ages in between, some of them pushed in baby carriages and others in wheelchairs; an old man barely able to put one foot in front of the other, several with handicaps challenging themselves to complete the distance… they helped comprise this human array.

I noticed walkers of different races and different national origins; and I mentally speculated that, were these thousands of participants polled, you'd find a wide spectrum of religious affiliations, political views, cultural beliefs, and economic circumstances. All of us, though, on this given morning had gathered here, together, and were sharing this experience.

With the possible exception of the domed state capitol building in Lansing, nothing pictorially symbolizes Michigan like the Mackinac Bridge. Yet they represent different symbols. While all Michiganders share the institution of government and are part of this representative democracy, the proceedings at the capitol seem to reflect and magnify that which divides us, emphasizing our differences rather than our similarities. Many of the men and women elected or appointed to occupy those corridors of power seem to hold more allegiance to their political party, ideology, special interest, social and economic groups, and to their personal background and vision, than to the common interests of the diverse melting pot of people who populate this state, and who they were elected to represent and to serve. I do not believe they act this way for any devious reasons (although there are probably a few exceptions to this generalization), but rather because the path of division and self-interest, propelled by the attitude of manning the barricades against any and all perceived foes, usually proves an easier route than finding a way to span the differences.

On this Labor Day, as I walk across this structure of steel and concrete, I see that the Mighty Mac does more than physically connect two masses of land, separated by a dark and choppy sea; the bridge also serves as a common ground, and a shared vision. Surrounding me on this walk were a multitude of hopes and aspirations, a cross section of the vibrancy, resiliency, and determination that undergirds this state. We did not all look alike, nor think alike, but the Mackinac Bridge belongs to each of us, and to all of us. It symbolizes that which connects us; a shared causeway for all of those aspirations and hopes; for all of the dreams of those who have journeyed across its graceful arc.

Indian Summer at Michigan State

Indian summer reigned supreme on the Saturday afternoon in early October when I decided to wander around the campus of Michigan State University. The trees looked resplendent in their reds and yellows with some browns mixed in, along with the remaining greenery. The bright sunlight filtering through the colorful canopy, the leaves stirring ever so slightly from a soft breeze, lent an enchantment to the setting.

Only a few students were out and about. A couple of them had parents in tow, no doubt showing them the sights. The football team had a bye-week. The rest of the students, I supposed, remained in their dormitory rooms, studying for an upcoming assignment, or recouping from their Friday-night entertainment; or else they had gone shopping at the nearby stores or had returned to their respective hometowns for the weekend.

I don't often drive into downtown East Lansing anymore. My regular travels across mid-Michigan take me along I-96, a roadway that skirts the southern edge of the campus. When I do drive westward on Grand River Highway, I usually go no further than Okemos before turning south towards the freeway and the more familiar route that takes me between home and work.

I needed a book though. Unable to locate the desired selection at the store in the Meridian Mall, I continued on Grand River until I reached East Lansing. Turning north off the main boulevard, I found a parking spot on Albert Street. The spot (by intention) was in front of the house I had lived in for a few months many, many moons ago. Zdan and I had shared the rent for the first-floor flat as each of us made one last stab at college life. I deposited enough coins in the meter to avoid a ticket (90 minutes is the maximum allowed) and walked over to the Barnes & Noble complex. After finding what I wanted, a purchase of just under ten dollars, I departed the store and headed across the street to the MSU Union.

Michigan State University was my stomping grounds for three years after high school graduation. I attended classes year-round until, within a few credits of becoming a senior, having run out of money, but more importantly, having lost any compelling ambition to continue, I departed. My initial intention was to return and earn the degree, and finish the unfinished task. But I never did.

I started out my freshman year as a political science major with an underlying desire to write. The writing would center on social issues and serve a political cause. When I left, I still harbored a desire to write, but was otherwise drifting. I had switched my major to philosophy, enjoying the introductory courses I had taken. Unfortunately for me, this field of study came under the purview of a Bachelor of Arts degree and required the successful completion of a year of foreign language. I stumbled badly in my Spanish class, and decided not to pursue this requirement. By doing so, I abandoned any chance at a high-minded academic career. A Bachelor of Science degree was more lenient on the matter of a foreign language, so I switched again, this time to Multidisciplinary Social Studies. That major was more to my liking, accommodating the varied mix of classes I had already taken. This curriculum was also, I realized even then, heavy on the general overview, and thin on any expertise or specialty training necessary to secure a job. I had chosen an easy path.

It took me awhile after college, and more than a few adventures and misadventures, to find a place to moor and then a heading to pursue. Journalism and then family have, together, provided responsibility and a direction. As luck would have it, the *potpourri* approach that I had taken while at MSU proved a good backdrop for weekly newspapering.

After quitting college, my next plan was to visit new places and experience exotic cultures. I had fallen under the spell of the Hemingway short story and the romance of the Lost Generation residing in Paris in the 1920s. The wish to see faraway places is one that many others, both young and old, share. I'd hoped that a prowess with the pen would serve as both a means and an end to this goal. I'd write about these interesting vistas, and the earnings from those compositions would fund the travels. That's a strategy many other would-be scribes have tried. A goodly number have actually succeeded.

Instead of traveling the world, I've wandered about Michigan whenever time and opportunity allowed. Otherwise, all in all, I haven't ventured too far geographically. What has finally mattered, career-wise, is the writing rather than movement: to hopefully have something worthwhile to report on, and something purposeful to comment about; to be engaged in this time and place rather than to drift aimlessly about, seeking sensation and stimulation rather than substance.

The return visits to my alma mater have been spaced out during these ensuing years despite my close proximity. On those occasions when I have come back, the visit has usually been spent, as this most recent excursion was, taking a stroll about the old part of the campus for a couple of hours, remembering those college days.

After leaving the Union building, I walked towards Beaumont Tower, then continued on past this campus landmark to the Agriculture Building and, still further on, towards Kedzie and Bessey Halls. The latter two were where I attended my first classes in Natural Science and American Thought & Language (ATL). Reaching a sidewalk that borders the Red Cedar River, I took the pathway eastward, going underneath Farm Lane Bridge to that wide expanse of lawn lying between the Auditorium and the Red Cedar. To the south, across the river, stood Shaw Hall, my home-away-from-home during my stay at MSU.

Here and there students, alone or in pairs, sat in the grass, reading a book or simply sunbathing. Most of them, I noticed, wore earplugs and were, I assume, listening to music as they reveled in the warmth of the day and the serenity of the surroundings. A few joggers passed by on this stretch of sidewalk; their effort at physical fitness being an appropriate complement to the larger purpose of this university; that purpose being to encourage and gratify the curiosity of the mind.

At age 60, my gray hair giving away any pretense of youth, I felt a tad out of place. If any of the youngsters noticed me, or cared enough to even wonder, they might have mistaken me for a professor who, like the joggers, was taking advantage of this fine day to get some needed exercise that would keep the muscles in shape. Or, perhaps, an astute one or two might have had me pegged correctly as a former student, one of many who return from time to time.

Still, even such a perceptive observer would be too young to notice (as I do) the faint whiff of a long-ago breeze, one that promised so much possibility. Nor would the young onlooker notice the barely discernible path, here on these grounds and amid these buildings, that once beckoned to me; a path which once stretched seemingly far into the horizon, but has now shortened considerably. Nor would any of them realize that for this gray-haired chap—like others of his generation—the greater distance now lies in retrospect rather than what might loom ahead.

I went past the Alumni Memorial Chapel; then, having reached Bogue Street, I headed north towards Snyder and Phillips Residential Halls, and finally circled back. A new art facility is being erected next to Grand River, joining the venerable and hallowed buildings long associated with this part of the campus, these classrooms where countless scholars, year after year, decade after decade, have learned their lessons. The construction project is a reminder that the needs of tomorrow must be served; that each year new students arrive as others depart. They, as I now do, will join the continuum of those who have strolled, or will stroll, across these grounds.

But 'the new' did not interest me on this autumn afternoon. I paused in front of Morrill Hall, taking a final look at the building. The structure, while looking quite sturdy and durable at first glance, will soon be destined for the wrecking ball. "Close monitoring of the internal wooden structure of the Hall has revealed irreparable deterioration, indicating that the more than 100-year-old building is approaching the end of its useful life" was the verdict reached by MSU officials that has determined its fate.

The philosophy department had been housed there when I attended, and I remember going inside to pick up a paper I'd written as part of my final grade. The essay, a comparison between Plato and David Hume, was the only one I saved from my college days.

Plato, the intellectual giant of ancient Athens, the writer who provided the foundation upon which Western thought has risen, famously stated that "Objects we observe or otherwise know through our sensory perceptions are merely copies or images of eternal ideas and these ideas (or forms) are the ultimate metaphysical realities, and therefore the object of true knowledge." He also stated that it was through the study of philosophy (i.e. obtaining true knowledge) and the use of logical reasoning that one could understand this eternal, otherwise indiscernible reality of ideal ideas.

From Platonism and its offspring Neo-Platonism was derived the philosophy of St. Augustine. Through his writings came several hundred years of accepted Christian Theology.

On the other hand, David Hume was a man from 18th century Scotland. He proved to be the ultimate of philosophical skeptics, and attempted to stand metaphysics on its head with his assertion: "I alone exist and the rest of the world is nothing more than a part of my consciousness," adding that "you cannot be certain something will always happen or exist in the future in the same way it has in the past; you cannot always determine that something will cause an effect."

He contended that without such certainty and stability about matter and being "we can prove nothing for certain, we can predict nothing, we cannot verify any real truth, even the self is hard to verify."

I suppose skepticism is not an altogether imprudent approach to this world, and our place in it. Far too many people are overly certain about all sorts of matters, firm and righteous in their belief, when such absolute conviction is not necessarily evident. The questioning mind, open to various possibilities and unafraid to test the waters, can take us to many places; whereas those who cling to the already-determined answers, who are reluctant or unwilling to go beyond the accepted and acceptable view, or who embrace an orthodoxy without question or reservation never leave the shore. Still, skepticism (that philosophy of uncertainty) is an endless circle of "what if, what if." At some point life needs to be moored to an acquired knowledge and belief; a solid dock from which to launch a voyage, and to return to after the exploration. If new knowledge necessitates a new mooring, then so be it; the quest for greater insight has been rewarded.

My walk on this afternoon took me back to the MSU Union and then to my car. I put the book on the passenger seat, looking forward to reading it. Like all of the other books I've obtained, a fair number of them while attending this university some forty years ago, the contents promise a new adventure.

My recollections of this place, however, are not only of bygone classes and books. Nor was my return on this day simply to revisit the once familiar walkways and buildings. Echoing in that faint breeze, stirring in the gently moving leaves, were the memories of long-ago friends, including the young ladies who, for a time, seemed to be the right one, and of all the rest of those with whom I shared this place and those brief years.

Their faces and voices, the laughter and occasional tears, the conversations that filled the hours and our hearts, all of the impending hopes and longings that permeated the setting… they simmer like a mirage in the far horizon. Their vividness, though, has slowly faded; my path has, alas, taken me too far away. In the yellow sunlight that filters through the colorful leaves, they seem more the stuff of dreams than a once-upon-a-time reality. But real they once were, and in my mind they still reside, and are still recalled with affection. They linger on as I do, and shall remain until memory disappears; the voices and faces drifting off like a wisp of autumn smoke as it ascends upwards towards the heavens. That, I suppose, is not the sentiment of a skeptic.

There exists a poignancy and bitter sweetness to an Indian summer afternoon. Opulent, almost aching in its beauty, we experience it, soaking in the sights and sounds, recalling similar moments like this one; yet we know it is fleeting, and impermanent. It's too compelling, a siren's call that, if followed, would take us off course. Like those long-ago memories, these final moments of a balmy season are soft reminders of what once was; the echoes of departure and of past tense. For a few moments you relish the splendor, look out at the simmering mirage until finally the necessity to move on returns. So, I head back to hearth and home, and back to the lady who has been and remains the right one. Back to where the journey still beacons, where the breeze of tomorrow still fills the sails; where the unwritten page awaits, and where each new day is another chance to be part of, and to influence, this time and place.

A Memory That Keeps Me Warm

During the years I was growing up, my great-grandparents, Rollin and Blanche Horton, lived on a 19-acre farm on West Allen Road. It was located about two miles north of Fowlerville. Along with the house, there was a red barn and a small narrow shed where the black '49 Ford was kept.

The place was referred to as "Uncle Jute's" by older relatives. Julius 'Jute' and Amarilla 'Rilly' Carr were Grandpa Rollin's uncle and aunt. They had owned this acreage as well as the larger farm across the road during the latter years of the 1800's and the early part of the 1900's. According to family lore, the Carrs lived in one of their homes during the summer and then stayed in the other house during the warm-weather months.

My great-grandparents sold their farm on Chase Lake Road to my grandparents, Lloyd and Ilah Mae, and moved in with Jute Carr to take care of him. Rilly had passed away, and he had become too old to stay alone. Somewhere along the line the larger farm had been sold. My great-grandparents assumed ownership of the remaining holding after Jute died.

The place where I grew up was about a mile-and-a-half away. I often pedaled my bike over there to visit. A few times, when we had our donkey, Dusty, I rode instead. Dusty, though, was a reluctant and unreliable form of transportation. He preferred not to wander too far from his stall. He was as likely to turn around after we'd ridden a half-mile or so, and gallop home, as he was to continue onward to the desired destination.

My mother or father, with us kids in tow, would often stop at my great-grandparents' place on our way to or from town. My father also farmed their land. So, between these various visits and stops, I spent a fair amount of time at their premises.

When I was quite young, Grandpa still had chickens. I remember getting up with him when I had spent the night, then going out to feed the hens and collect their eggs in the morning. I vaguely recall watching him butcher several chickens one afternoon. The image of his chopping off the bird's head with his ax, followed by the chicken running about the yard with blood squirting out its neck, proved an indelible one.

Grandpa's arthritis began to slowly limit his mobility. While he kept busy doing tasks and while he still drove his Ford into town, over to the cemetery, or to the home of a relative, more and more I'd see him in a rocker. He had a chair in the kitchen; the spot where I'd usually find him. But during the winter, he occupied a good portion of the day in the back room. A stove sat in the far corner, with the split wood stacked against the wall. His chair was strategically situated in front of the stove and next to the wood. Whenever the heat began to dissipate, he'd open the door and carefully put in a chunk or two of firewood. When not tending to the fire, he read, looked out the window, or visited with me (or whoever might have stopped). With all of the family and long-time neighbors in the vicinity, my great-grandparents enjoyed plenty of company.

The past few mornings it's been chilly when I've gotten up. The cooler version of fall has arrived. We have one of those super-duper space heaters that, as advertised, warms up a good portion of the surrounding area. We keep it in the living room where we have a pair of rockers, and where I start off my day with coffee and writing down the list of things I plan to accomplish during the next few hours. From my rocker I can look out the large picture window at the lawn and roadway. Beyond this sight is the neighboring farm with its buildings and fields. One day each week I use this time to scribble my thoughts on a legal pad, conjuring up yet another column. Like the three witches in *Macbeth*, I mix up my brew. Will it be insightful and lively? A potent concoction? "Fair is foul and foul is fair," the ladies chanted. That might describe my writing style as well.

A second space heater is located in the adjacent family room, next to the television; the part of our house where I spend most of my evenings. This model possesses fewer bells and whistles than the super-duper one, doesn't produce as much heat, but still manages to provide adequate comfort.

We have central heat (propane); however, our home, like many others, offers more living space than needed. Since we prefer cooler temperatures when sleeping, are away from the house a good part of each day, and have an aversion to expensive heating bills, the thermostat is kept at a modest setting. The portable heaters, like Grandpa Rollin's wood stove, fill the void. I put one close to my rocker and all is well. If there's still a little too much chill for the liking, I can wrap an afghan around my legs.

A rocking chair, a warm fire, a window view of the countryside, along with some entertaining and interesting reading, occasional conversation, and a few moments to ponder, contemplate, and rest easy; I'm reminded of their value when the cold winds of winter begin to blow.

Grandpa Rollin was 96 when he passed away in his sleep. I had turned 24. Of all my countless memories of him, of all our times together, remembering him in that room on those long-ago afternoons remains my favorite. I thought about him again on this early morning when the chill air in the living room prompted me to turn on the heater. I thought about him sitting in that back room of Uncle Jute's, the fire burning in the stove, and the pile of split wood. It is a memory that still keeps me warm.

Tom Braun: A Man with Heart

In tribute to my friend who died in 2011

The year was 1976. I had been hired earlier by the *Livingston County Press* as its Fowlerville area correspondent, providing news and features. I was being paid $5 per article, thus when an editor from the *Lansing State Journal* contacted me, asking if I'd like to provide that paper with Fowlerville news as well, I felt elated. My prospects, languishing since leaving college four years before, seemed to be brightening. Freelance work for the *Journal*, I thought, might lead to a fulltime position with that daily.

I met the gentleman for lunch. He offered pointers, told me I'd get $100 a month if I produced a certain number of articles, and then drove me about town, suggesting some ideas for feature stories. One of the places we went was to the Fowlerville Fairgrounds. He was less than complimentary about the condition of the place, a comment that startled me since, like many of my fellow townspeople, I took pride in this venerable institution.

He decided I should do a story, detailing (in his opinion) the sad state of the grounds, and how this deterioration had been allowed to occur. While I could see two or three of the livestock barns had gotten 'long in the tooth', they didn't look much worse than a couple of buildings on the family farm where I'd grown up. But I nodded my head to his request. Later, I wondered if this had been premeditated rather than a spur-of-the-moment command.

I knew that Tom Braun, operator of Braun Cleaners, served as the Fair Secretary, but other than knowing what he looked like, I had never met him. Someone had told me he could be hard-edged. A couple of days later, with trepidation about my covert mission and expecting a hard-edged reception, I went to the Cleaners, introduced myself (although he knew who I was), and told him that the *State Journal* wanted me to do a story on how the fair operated; a behind-the-scenes look, if you will. I did not mention it was supposed to be a critical *expose*.

The request excited him. His enthusiasm made me feel guilty about the ulterior purpose. The next day I met him at the fair office for the interview. He had brought along Bill Miner, a longtime fair board member. I learned about the 'nuts and bolts' of how fair week was organized, starting with the January state convention when entertainment was booked, followed by the production of the annual Fair Premium Book, and also about the ongoing maintenance and improvement projects being done on the buildings and grounds to get them ready for the early July event.

I learned, as well, about a group of dedicated people who had, since the 1950s when the fair seemed on the brink of demise, worked hard to keep things going. Bill Miner noted that there had been a point when the board offered to give the fair to the county: an offer that was turned down by the Board of Supervisors, and that a couple of times loans from private individuals were all that kept the fair operating for another year.

But by 1976, Tom informed me, the financial picture had steadily improved for a number of years, and the surplus money was being used to catch up with infrastructure enhancements: like installing new water and sewer lines and expanding the electrical service capacity. He noted that the new fair office we were sitting in was a much-needed accomplishment and that eventually the board planned to fix up or replace the older barns and other buildings. In his remarks, Tom kept focusing the credit for these successes towards the other board members. Later, I'd be told by those fair officials that Tom, as secretary and fair manager, deserved a good measure of praise as well.

Warming up during our interview, and as we discussed this comeback, Tom made a statement that crystallized the message I was hearing… "What has kept the fair going over the years, what keeps it going each year are all of the people who donate their time, talents, and energy in all kinds of ways," he said, adding, "Volunteers are the heart of the Fowlerville Fair."

That latter quotation was the lead as well as the headline of the article I submitted to the *State Journal*. The ensuing narrative, rather than being a hatchet job, had a celebratory tone. To the editor's credit he published the story as I'd written it. I suspected, though, that he was disappointed with my decision. I did other stories during the next few months, mostly reporting on the village council and school board meetings. There were a few articles, ones with more legitimately controversial topics, that resulted in banner headlines on the paper's state news page, along with several 'feel good' features that were spotlighted. But apparently my output didn't cause a great impression. I was informed that, due to budget concerns that necessitated a cutback in free-lance staff, my services would no longer be needed.

My hopes of landing a full-time job with the daily (as a result of this opportunity) ended. Meanwhile, I'd been submitting the same or similar articles to the *Livingston County Press,* and the editor of that publication was quite happy with my output. He even bumped me up to $10 an article and eventually I secured a full-time position with this newspaper. Despite a few twists and turns along the way, my career has been in weekly newspaper journalism.

What I discovered, although it took awhile for me to understand, was that my loyalty, as well as the kind of journalism I preferred to pursue, lay with that celebratory article rather than the requested critical piece. "Two paths," to borrow the metaphor from the Robert Frost poem, and in my case, the choice I made after my interview with Tom Braun made a great difference in my life.

What I also discovered at that interview was a man— about 12 years older than me— who was friendly and engaging. It was the start of a wonderful friendship that grew and flourished and would include 'his' Dawn and their children— Kurt, Keri, and Kami— along with others in their circle of family and friends.

On a professional level I would eventually do PR work for the fair; then later I was in charge of organizing and printing the Fair Book. For several years, 'my' Dawn and I, through the sponsorship of the *Fowlerville News & Views,* put on the Ladies Day Program. In addition, Braun Cleaners was always a supportive advertiser of this newspaper until Tom closed his business in 2005 and retired.

On a personal level, the first 10 years I had the Brauns to myself. Then, after taking a job in Hastings, I returned one afternoon during fair week, accompanied by a lady I was engaged to, and introduced her. Tom and Dawn figuratively embraced her. Still later, when our son Bradley was born, they became Uncle Tom and Aunt Dawn. Keri babysat him one summer when he was a toddler and accompanied him on his first fair ride. After that Kami took over and for many summers, until he became a teenager and no longer needed such oversight, he was a fixture at the Braun household. What started out as two guys talking about the fair in a newspaper interview, over the ensuing years blossomed into a friendship and shared affection between two families.

I have a multitude of memories about Tom. It's impossible to adequately convey the wide scope. I remember the Monday mornings when I'd stop at the Cleaners to leave that week's papers to be distributed, usually ten of them, and we'd spend a few minutes visiting. He was knowledgeable, thoughtful, and opinionated on all manner of topics. More than once our conversations put me behind schedule, but the chats were worth the delay.

There are memories from all of those fair weeks over the years; of seeing him in action. Other recollections include our two families visiting one of Tom's favorite places, the Detroit Zoo; seeing his pride in the railroad diorama he'd set up in his basement; the restaurant meals we shared; the weddings of his children; the year he and Dawn were Santa and Mrs. Claus at the Christmas Parade; the year they were honored as the parade's Grand Marshals; the fun we had at the fair conventions in Grand Rapids; and seeing the warm bantering between his mother Luella and him at the Cleaners.

Most of all I remember his friendliness, his smile, his good-natured teasing, his bulldog determination (yes, he could be hard-edged in standing up for what he believed), his anger when he felt someone was abusing a trust or acting in an unethical or improper manner, and his love for and pride in his family. As the Fair Secretary and in other aspects of his life, he behaved and acted with integrity. He was not self-important nor did he seek personal benefit from his position. Instead, his inclination was to include others, shift the spotlight and credit to them whenever he could, and bring people together for a common purpose. I don't wish to paint him as a saint. Like all of us, there were mistakes, misjudgments, and an ill-advised word, but in the larger sum his life, the manner in which he lived, the standards and morals that guided him, I found him to be an admirable gentleman.

Tom and I did not see as much of each other after he retired. We could have, but most of us get involved in our personal orbits, caught up in regular routines that seem to quickly fill up our days. That's not an excuse, just a weak explanation. It's at a moment like this, the sudden death of an old and dear friend, that you regret not making an effort to spend more time together. Still, I'll have this host of warm recollections—and for that I'm grateful.

One of those memories is running into Tom at the Little Glad Center over a year ago. I was leaving papers off for distribution there, and I spied him walking along the hall with his grandson, Grant. The two of them were holding hands and talking to each other, Tom bent down to better hear what the boy was saying. "Grandpa Tom," I thought, as hard-edged as a teddy bear. My great sadness, besides losing my friend, is that six youngsters have lost their wonderful grandfather.

He instilled in me two main ideas. The first is that involvement in a community event or institution (like the Fowlerville Fair) is not about self-promotion or self-benefit, or having an egotistical attitude, but is instead about being part of a larger effort, and shared purpose. "There is no single individual who does everything," he once said. "It takes a group effort. That's what makes a community." The other is that having a position, like being manager of the fair, is both a trust and responsibility. He had great respect and regard for the older generation that had operated the fair, kept it going and prospering, and felt that was his duty and charge to follow that example. By doing so, he instilled that ethic in a younger group, including myself.

A torch had been passed to him (this job of managing the fair), and Tom took great care in keeping that flame glowing, then finally passing it on. He had many reasons to feel a sense of pride and accomplishment in his life, his family being the primary one, but I believe that his long tenure at the fair was near the top of that list. Long ago, at our first meeting, he had told me that "Volunteers were the heart of the Fowlerville Fair." What I came to learn, in part from his example, is that volunteering in unison with others is the heart of many of our successful endeavors. The caveat is that when you give of yourself, you do so with care, compassion, and integrity of purpose.

That said, for me there'll always be another "Heart of the Fowlerville Fair." It belonged to a fellow who was a bit on the short and stocky side. I can picture him, wearing a ball cap, a twinkle in his eye, as he walked about the grounds, conversing with all those who shared in that common effort. Tom Braun was a man with heart.

A Christmas Carol: Still Relevant

The tale is a familiar one. It's about three "spirits" who visit a businessman on three successive December nights in London. In the course of those visits, the gentleman re-considers his views on Christmas, the poor, and the manner in which he has lived his life.

Charles Dickens wrote *A Christmas Carol* in 1843, with that businessman being Ebenezer Scrooge. A later writer called the novel "the second greatest story ever told," the first being the chronicle about Jesus; his birth in Bethlehem, his ministry, crucifixion, and resurrection. Dickens, with this story, was credited with helping to re-institute many of the secular trappings of the holiday celebration… "Making merry." Those trappings, popularized in Great Britain, soon found their way to America.

Dickens said that he had initially planned to write a pamphlet critical of "the British government changes to the welfare system known as the 'Poor Laws'." A destitute applicant, as a last resort, could go to a Poor House where he was required to work on a treadmill. That contraption was not an exercise device, although the user burned plenty of calories. The treadmills, going in continuous circles, ground grain or pumped up water.

Saying that the worker "burned calories," however, would be misleading since not a lot of food was provided to create them. The government, evoking that convenient human logic called 'rationalization', did not wish for the Poor House to be more attractive than other alternatives. So the amount of food and other necessities was deliberately limited. Nor could the residents accept outside aid. Throw in a little graft and greed on the part of the administrators of these institutions, and the resulting living and working conditions proved harsh. According to historical reports, many people, despite being poor, did not resort to this alternative; not that this meant the situation was necessarily any better for them elsewhere. Private and religious charities, along with trade unions, then as now, attempted to help.

A Christmas Carol (it's also been stated) "was an indictment of nineteenth century capitalism." Prior to the crafting of the book, the Luddite Movement had come and gone. This was an effort by many English workers, mainly tradesmen in the wool and textile industries, to stop the development of industrialization in the early 1800s. They did so by destroying or sabotaging the machines. The reaction by these workers was fueled in part by the loss of their trades, the deteriorating working conditions in the factories, low wages, and the unwillingness of the government to help them. British justice, in reaction, was swift and merciless. Several were hung while others were deported to the penal colonies.

The 1840s was also the tail end of the 'Parliamentary Enclosure of the English Commons'. Enclosure was the term used to describe the process, approved by the Parliament, where land, which had been previously shared by everyone in the rural villages, was given instead to private owners. While this process had been occurring in spurts since the 1500s, it accelerated after the mid-1700s. The shift was from communal to individual agriculture, and the individuals who gained this property were mainly landowners already well-off, who utilized tenant farmers to do the heavy lifting. This privatization of the land resulted in the abolition of grazing and planting rights to common lands that the villagers had previously enjoyed. Accelerating this trend were advances in labor-saving farming equipment and the introduction of crop rotation and other science-based applications that improved yields.

The end result was that 'subsistence farming' gave way to more efficient agricultural practices that created surplus commodities and profitable returns on investment, yet needed fewer workers. While this trend allowed many well-connected landowners, including the aristocracy and gentry, to become even richer, many ordinary folk, having had this right to the commons taken away and no longer being needed as agricultural workers, found themselves caught between the proverbial rock and the hard place. According to the historical accounts, "They left the rural areas to move into the cities where they became laborers in the Industrial Revolution."

Aiding and abetting these social changes was the growth of the British Empire. Great Britain imported raw materials from its colonies or zones of influence, created manufactured goods, and shipped them back to those colonies, and elsewhere in the world. The British army maintained order in those far flung locales, while the British Navy protected the sea lanes from other nations and pirates. As noted, some of the displaced population ended up in these colonies. Many of the younger men, meanwhile, were conscripted into or joined the military, while others (men, women, and children) manned the growing industrial complex. The surplus in food helped to maintain the existing population level. Later, improved production methods would help sustain a steady growth in the British population. As this process was unfolding, there was a concern expressed by some British intellectuals, most notably Thomas Malthus, that not enough resources existed, particularly land and food, to maintain "a surplus population."

The economy, then as now, operated in cycles of boom and bust. That was even more noticeable with the advent of the Industrial Revolution. Back in the early 1800s when the factories shut down or laid off workers, without much of a safety net in place, the workers had to fend for themselves. Throw in the facts that vagrancy (the lack of a home) was a crime, that the inability to pay your debts could land you in debtor's prison (which had happened to Dickens' father), along with the situation of many people no longer able to produce their own food, and 'Merry Old England' during that time period was not a pleasant place to reside if a person was without work or some other means of support. The British government's remedy, as noted, was the Poor House; a place where the meals were meager and the day was spent working on the treadmill.

Dickens wanted his readers "to recognize the plight of those whom the Industrial Revolution had displaced and driven into poverty and the obligation of society to provide for them humanely."

"Failure to do so," Dickens implies through the personification of *Ignorance and Want* as ghastly children in his novel, "will result in an unnamed 'Doom' for those who believe their wealth and status qualify them to sit in judgment of the poor, rather than to assist them."

Great Britain did not suffer 'Doom.' The nation avoided that fate, in part, because the wealthy are resourceful at protecting themselves, as often as not through their use of governmental power, but more so because the treatment of the poor became (as Dickens hoped) more just, and because the workers were able to share some of the wealth created by the growth of a manufacturing economy. In Great Britain, this segment of the population is called the 'working class', while in this country we prefer the term 'middle class'.

The current situation in Michigan is not as dire and desperate as what Dickens depicted in his famous story. For those who are out-of-work, and find themselves slipping into poverty, and for those who have always struggled for assorted reasons to scrounge up enough money to survive, help does exist—both governmental and charitable. But the attitude about money and the antipathy towards the poor and the displaced have familiar echoes.

In place of the Industrial Revolution, we have Globalization. While there are benefits to this emerging world economy and free flow of trade, a definite ill effect for our state has been the loss of tens of thousands of good-paying manufacturing jobs. This loss has taken place due to companies deciding it was more efficient and profitable to relocate their operations in other countries where labor is much cheaper, union protection of workers is non-existent, environmental concerns are ignored, and taxes that help provide social amenities and protections for the citizenry are lower.

The loss of jobs has also been due to the steady use of automation, with highly-technical machines replacing manual labor; and, of course, the 'bust cycle' that took place for much of the past decade had a crippling effect on Michigan. It could be argued, borrowing the line from Dickens, that the state has "a surplus population" given the current situation: too many would-be workers for the number of existing jobs and too many of those jobs requiring the sort of skills that many of these workers do not yet possess.

What has been occurring in Lansing during the past several months has been a shrinking and altering of the social service programs that were designed to assist those who find themselves in rough circumstances. The cuts and curtailments are not necessarily major, *unless* you are the person or family being cut and curtailed. Some of the changes, in fairness, are prudent. Some of them will not occur in the immediate future. Still, the overall trend is to push people out of these protective programs, and to withdraw such help from future recipients or severely limit their eligibility. The restrictions in eligibility and reductions in monetary aid, either already approved or proposed, include food stamps, financial assistance to impoverished families, unemployment benefits, and workers compensation.

What can also occur is the slow dulling of the sensibilities about the plight of the poor or disadvantaged, a coarsening of compassion and a loss of empathy. The realization that "there but for the grace of God go I" gives way to Social Darwinism —"a survival of the fittest"— in the competition for available resources. The all-to-easy inclination is to blame people for their dire situation, rather than to take into account the possible circumstances that caused it. This can be seen in the comments of legislators who defend the changes with comments that "We don't want welfare to be a lifestyle," implying that the poor enjoy being poor, and "Extensions of unemployment benefits encourage people not to seek a job," insinuating that many laid-off workers prefer an idle life to gainful employment.

It's an attitude akin to that shown by Scrooge when he was asked by the two gentlemen, early in the story, to donate to charity. Scrooge asked, "Are there no prisons? And the Union workhouses? Are they still in operation? The Treadmill and the Poor Law are in full vigor then?"

The gentlemen answered, "Many can't go there; and many would rather die."

To which Scrooge retorted, "If they would rather die, they had better do it, and decrease the surplus population."

From Dickens' point-of-view, government policy, in league with great wealth, was ignoring and victimizing those less fortunate. Money and its accumulation, for Scrooge and his real-life nineteenth century counterparts, were more important than the well being of their fellow men and women.

Certainly, there are deadbeats who would rather be on the public dole than work. Certainly, there are loopholes in Michigan's system that allow (or have allowed) some people to take advantage of the system, obtaining money and other help they are not qualified to get, nor should be getting. Certainly, the goal is to help get individuals and families off of this assistance, to become more self-sufficient, and not make it "a way of life." But this is only one side of the coin. The examples of abuse and misuse are more anecdotal than symptoms of a widespread and systematic problem.

Making "ends meet" in our modern American society is not a cheap nor easy proposition. Food, housing, transportation, gas, insurance, clothing, medical care, and all of the odds-and-ends of day-to-day living add up. Couple that challenge with an official unemployment rate that is currently over 10 percent, an actual jobless number that (experts tell us) is substantially higher, plus numerous instances where a lot of the unemployed and under-employed are single mothers with young children, and it's hard in my mind to support a policy that takes away or shrinks protection and assistance, rather than buttresses this public help.

We hear the constant trumpet call of lower taxes, cutting government spending, and the need to make Michigan more "business friendly." That's all well and good. Encouraging business and private enterprise is indeed important to our economic well-being. Overly burdensome government, multi-layered government, bloated government… whatever you wish to call it, does exist to an extent. It seems to be human nature, in its civilized form, to create institutions, along with rules and regulations that are complex. Yet government, as we've established it in this nation and in this state, is, as Lincoln reminded us, "of the people, by the people, and for the people." It is *us*, not an enemy, not a parasite, and not simply *the problem*.

Over the long decades of practice and of trial-and-error, government has been found to be the best means to educate our young, build roads and necessary public infrastructure, protect us from criminals and malcontents, defend us from foreign enemies, regulate the rules of trade, aid and abet economic development, and help us survive and recover from natural disasters. Government has also proven to be the most logical means to assist the widow and orphan, the elderly, the physically and mentally handicapped, the sick and the infirm, and yes, even the poor and temporarily displaced. There are different terms to describe these various roles, including safety net, social welfare, and public works, but perhaps the most appropriate is the Constitutional language of "providing the common defense and promoting the common good."

The 'Spirits of Christmas Past, Present, and Future' were not the only visitors Scrooge had on that long ago Christmas season. His old partner Marley, dragging a length of chain, was the first one to appear. He came to warn Scrooge that their obsession with money was a mistaken priority. Marley spoke of "life's opportunity missed" and "regret" and said, "My spirit never walked beyond our counting house — mark me— in life my spirit never roved beyond the narrow limits of our money-changing hole."

When Ebenezer observed, with a bit of affection, "But you were always a good man of business, Jacob," the ghost cried out in his now well-known reply…

"Business. Mankind was my business. The common welfare was my business; charity, mercy, forbearance, and benevolence, were all my business. The dealings of my trade were but a drop of water in the comprehensive ocean of my business!"

A Christmas Carol is a story of redemption and re-direction; a reminder of what truly is the important business of life and living. While the plot may be set in a now long-ago time and place, its message is as important, compelling, and fresh as today's headlines. People, those around us, are not the means to an end; that end being the making of money, the accumulation of wealth, and a dog-eat-dog struggle to remain on top of the economic heap. People should not be viewed or treated as cogs in the machinery, some beast of burden used to turn the treadmill. Mankind is our business, so when we refer to the common welfare, it is *not* just for you or me and *not* just for those who are well off—the more fortunate— but for each and all.

"God bless us," Dickens wrote in the book's final line, "Every One!"

(Written in December 2011)

Pure Michigan on Hall Lake

A *Pure Michigan* summer afternoon. I drove along Gun Lake Road until I reached the public access for Hall Lake. I turned into the lot, found a parking spot, and unloaded the fishing gear. Then, with pole and pail in hand, I followed a narrow, worn path into a dense cover of woods, walking gingerly along this crevice-like opening amid the trees and underbrush. Finally, I spotted a small clearing.

But not much of clearing. Just enough room to cast my line. More importantly, though, this stretch of lake did not have a thick growth of lily pads in the shallow waters that hugged the shoreline. There were weeds visible several feet under the surface, but enough water above them that I felt I could fish without my hook getting caught constantly in the undergrowth.

I was not the first fisherman to find this spot, and its advantages. Evidence showed that the site was well used. After a few casts, followed by some adjustments to the length of line below the bobber, and my hopes were rewarded with a nibble. Another few casts and I landed a decent bluegill. I anticipated a fine outing on these waters.

When people talk of picturesque, particularly the gorgeous *Pure Michigan* outdoors' scenes, this pristine lake would top any list. Modest in size, it is surrounded by high bluffs of hardwoods and pines; and boasts a tiny island. Today, in the bright sun of late afternoon, the greenery was lush and vibrant, while parts of the lake's surface sparkled like a field of diamonds from the reflected sunlight. Overhead was a nearly cloudless aqua-colored sky.

Hall Lake is part of the 5,000-acre Yankee Springs Recreation Area in western Barry County. Better known and more popular is the portion of the Recreation Area that borders nearby Gun Lake, the third largest inland body of water in our state. The word 'borders' though is not quite accurate. Rather the state campground and its adjacent day-use area are located on a long, slightly crooked finger of land that pokes out into the lake. Here, each year, thousands of families pitch their tents or park their travel trailers and stay for awhile. Thousands more utilize the remainder of this peninsula to swim or sunbath, picnic, launch their boats, bicycle, take a stroll, or even fish.

A few miles away is found the more primitive Deep Lake Campground that, despite its lack of modern amenities, is another popular choice. Near that is the Horsemen's Campground where the equine crowd can bring their trusty steeds, camp, and ride along the marked trails.

For me, despite a multitude of people in the general vicinity, Hall Lake (itself) proved to be a place of quiet and solitude. To my right, on the far end of the lake, a pair of fellow angers had the convenience of a motor boat. They appeared to be seeking bass. Two sets of kayakers were also using the lake, but none of them chose to row their yellow-colored vessels near me.

Over the next two hours my expectations of success, brought on by that first strike, were tempered. I had plenty of bites: several times the bobber disappeared beneath the surface. For a moment, when this occurred, I felt confident that I had caught one. But apparently these Hall Lake fish are a crafty bunch. Most of them managed to avoid my efforts to set the hook. I only managed to catch two runts, neither of them worth keeping. Instead, I tossed them back into the lake to gain girth.

Finally, near the end of my outing, I landed another decent-sized bluegill. I had just told myself that if I got a fish with this cast, I'd leave. But I didn't, reasoning that "Maybe, with the sun going down and the day cooling off, they're starting to feed." With that in mind, ever the opportunist, I tossed out my baited line once more. And again. And again. Then I landed another gill. "One more," I figured, "and I'll have enough for a meal."

My persistence paid off when, like a bolt out of the blue, I felt a hard tug, set the hook with a quick backward flick, and knew instantly that I'd caught that fourth fish. From the force of the pull against the pole I began to suspect I'd found even more success.

"Yes!" I mentally shouted as my catch neared. "A bass!"

After taking out the hook, I put my prize into the pail of water that I'd set next to me, only a couple of feet from the shore. From where I had set the bucket, to the nearby water's edge, the shore sloped downwards about 45 degrees. That placement turned out to be a problem.

As I prepared to leave, the bass pushed itself out of the pail. "Oh, no, he's going to get away!" I thought as I saw him flopping. When I reached to grab him, I knocked over the pail and now, suddenly, the three other fish were flopping about. I caught the bass (this time by hand), and tossed it up next to a tree. I then located one of the bluegills. As I grabbed it, out of the corner of my eye, I saw movement going down the slope and heard a faint "plunk" of something disturbing the water.

I searched the immediate area, but found neither of the other two fish. They'd escaped. I noticed then that one of my tennis shoes was soaked from the spilled water and had become covered with sand.

After putting my remaining fish (also coated with sand) into the pail, I retraced my steps on the narrow path back to the car.

Yes, it was a *Pure Michigan* afternoon, complete with the sort of visual feast of scenery that the copy writers employ for their marketing efforts. But I doubt they'd include the part about the hapless fisherman.

Facing 'Hard Stuff': Coleman Young's Story Offers Lesson

Coleman A. Young ended his tenure as mayor of Detroit in 1993. Shortly afterwards, he published an autobiography (with the help of Lonnie Wheeler) entitled *Hard Stuff*.

A few weeks ago I came across the book while perusing the shelves of my local library. Given what was happening with the proposed (planned) state takeover of the city's government via the Emergency Financial Manager Law—a proposal that became a reality this past week (March 2013) when Gov. Rick Snyder pulled the trigger—I thought the contents might be enlightening.

How prescient of me.

Mayor Young's life story, along with the opinions and observations that peppered the narrative, proved fascinating and compelling. He had a reputation for being profane at times (meaning he swore in polite company) and hard-edged in his dealings. Given the incidents of unfairness and harassment he faced while growing up in a segregated society; a time when African Americans were frequently confined to certain crowded neighborhoods and often felt the metaphorical boot on the neck when it came to jobs, schools, police, and social advancement, his attitude and responses seem understandable.

"Feisty" would be an appropriate description of his personality. He looked racism and racists in the eye, refusing to blink or shift his gaze in submission. He went toe-to-toe with the U.S. House Committee on Un-American Activities when he was subpoenaed to testify in 1952 because of his union-organizing activities. He had a critical opinion about 'bleeding heart' liberals who opposed his economic development efforts during his tenure as mayor, and a less-than-flattering view of the Detroit media.

Concerning the latter, he felt Detroit's two daily newspapers (the *Free Press* and *News*) and TV newscasts preferred sensationalism to a fair and objective consideration of facts when it came to covering his administration. He felt they played up the idea that Detroit was dysfunctional and crime-ridden, thereby catering to a receptive audience in the adjacent suburbs, and were willing accomplices to federal prosecutors who sought to tarnish his reputation through selective leaks during a couple of high-profile investigations into alleged corruption.

The latter portion of his autobiography— a detailed re-telling of the highs and lows of his 20 years as mayor— was certainly his attempt to "set the record straight" (as he viewed that record) at the moment he was stepping off the public stage and would no longer be in the limelight. He sought to explain and justify his actions and motives as well as give his interpretation on what happened. In the final pages Young talks about his decision to not seek a sixth four-year term), and mentions some health issues. He was 75 years old at the time. As it turned out, he passed away just four years later; thus the book proved to be a final testament.

While aware that this book served as his explanation and version of events, I nevertheless found myself sympathetic to the challenges and predicaments he faced as head of Michigan's largest and best-known city.

And what were those challenges and overall predicaments?

Well, foremost has been the redistribution of population and wealth from the city to the outlying areas. In news stories about the current financial abyss faced by the city, the population decline is prominently mentioned. At the start of the 1950s, with Detroit having prospered during World War II as the 'Arsenal of Democracy' and poised to enjoy an explosion of automotive purchases, that number stood at 1.8 million.

Over the next two decades white residents began moving to the suburbs. The exodus accelerated in the late 1960s after the '67 riot and then in the early 1970s when the federal courts attempted to integrate schools through busing. At the time of Young's election as mayor in 1973, the population had dropped to below 1.5 million and was around 1.2 million in 1980. The population decline has continued its free fall since then, and is now pegged at around 700,000.

"It's mind boggling to think that, at mid-century, Detroit was a city of close to two million and nearly everything beyond its borders was covered with corn and cow patties," Young noted in the book. "Forty years later, damn near every last white person in the city had moved to the old fields and pastures— 1.4 frigging million of them. Think about that. There were 1,600,000 white people in Detroit after the war, and 1,400,000 of them left. By 1990, the city was just over a million, nearly eighty percent was black, and the suburbs had surpassed Detroit not only in population, but in wealth, (and) in commerce."

This exodus of residential and business wealth, this relocation of shopping centers and factories into previous open spaces, left Detroit city government, including Mayor Young and the ensuing administrations, with a severe structural problem.

There was still the necessity to operate a city that covers 138.75 square miles; to provide police and fire protection, water and sanitation services, street maintenance and lights, and garbage pickup; but without a solid foundation of property taxes, and with a dwindling amount of state revenue sharing funds due to fewer and fewer residents.

Detroit, on the eve of Young's first election, had become a black-majority city, yet decades of discrimination in jobs, housing, education, and business opportunities had left many of those African American residents without the same financial and institutional resources that the city had enjoyed when its 1.8 million people worked at all of those now defunct stores and factories.

Another major challenge for Young was integrating the police force. He, and many blacks, viewed the Detroit cops, including the infamous STRESS unit, as a hostile force. And with good reason.

The roots of the social conflicts and tensions date back to the early 1900s when Henry Ford and the other early auto makers' offer of good-paying jobs brought thousands of newcomers to the city. The 'great melting pot' that resulted, and grew over the ensuing decades—a combination that included Eastern European nationalities, Appalachian whites, and Deep South blacks—did not mix well at times. In the prevailing hierarchy that emerged, blacks occupied the lowest rungs of the ladder. They had the worst jobs in the auto plants, and were the lowest paid. They found limited job opportunities elsewhere other than menial, service-oriented occupations. Even so, as Young relates in his book and from his personal experiences, there was resentment, and sometimes a violent reaction, to any accomplishments and advancements by blacks.

The police, made up almost entirely of white officers, was used to enforce the economic and social *status quo*. In too many instances, Young pointed out, patrolmen resorted to violent behavior against black citizens.

Mayor Young's persistent effort to bring equality to the Detroit Police Department, and to root out unprofessional behavior, was not, to put it mildly, met with open arms by the officers or the police union. His enforcement of the residency law—which required city employees to live in the city, but which had not been strictly enforced—was likewise greeted with hostility.

In the view of many whites, this effort was reverse discrimination and an imposition of racial quotas. Young, on the other hand, felt that integrating black officers into the force, thereby creating a racial parity number-wise, was a long-overdue remedy, both in terms of fairness and in lessening the tensions between the police and the community. He used similar reasoning in bringing a substantial number of women into the ranks.

Young saw jobs as the key to Detroit's long-term viability and to the prosperity of its residents. With this goal in mind, he put a priority on revitalizing both the Downtown and Riverfront areas through public-and-private development, efforts that resulted in the Renaissance Center and the Joe Louis Arena. In the 1980s a new General Motors auto manufacturing factory in Poletown and a new Chrysler assembly plant on the city's east side became realities. "Major industrial redevelopment was absolutely necessary for the economic survival of Detroit," he said of those initiatives.

But while he sought to keep industrial jobs in the city, and create new ones through redevelopment, Young was a realist. He pointed out that most of the factories and jobs existed outside the city limits. He saw clearly that the reconfiguration of population had resulted in a large entity called Metro Detroit, including Detroit and all of the suburbs, and that a cooperative regional approach was advisable. Still, important as this was, he felt that any cooperative effort needed to be fair to both the city and the suburbs.

To that end, he pushed for a light-rail system and other rapid transit options that would better connect the overall region. He further contended that these transportation links would more firmly bind the city and suburbs together socially and economically, spurring additional development. He reasoned that people in Detroit, unable to afford cars, needed this option to commute to the available work outside the city. At the same time, he felt the outlying suburbs would prosper by this convenient access to the city, with its assorted amenities and potential. You might say it was another version of the economic idea that "a rising tide carries all ships."

Unfortunately, his attempts to promote rapid transit met with resistance. Perhaps his feistiness did not help. The idea is still with us, most recently pushed by Gov. Snyder, and so is the resistance. The opposition, according to Young, came in two main forms: first was the opinion that the system would be another government freebie for Detroit blacks, and second, if there was to be a mass-transit system, suburban officials should be in control.

His other efforts to foster a regional approach, in his view, suffered a similar fate for the same reasons. According to Young, the suburbs saw such co-operation as coming at their expense; or, they wanted to take over Detroit's assets, including its water system, parks, and cultural institutions. "The suburbs' drive to control Detroit is an impetus that we've had to continually resist," he stated in the book.

Still, despite these attitudes and obstacles, and the failure of several co-operative attempts, Mayor Young still believed as he left office that a shared approach was and would be in the best interest of everyone. A vibrant Detroit, he said, would enhance the surrounding communities and the rest of Michigan. Furthermore, what was true for his town and state, he felt was valid for other urban areas in the nation.

"There must be a widespread recognition of the fact that America can only be as strong as its most troubled areas—its cities," he said in the book. "There must be a goal shared commonly between all jurisdictions and races, that (goal) being the achievement of full employment and equal opportunity for all."

Young said that this goal was a bedrock principle he held throughout his time as mayor; and before that as a state senator and as a union organizer; one he sought to accomplish through a combination of racial balance, affirmative action, and economic development.

He called it "playing the equality card."

Detroit, having been judged as unable to fix its financial and budgetary problems, is now under the control of Gov. Snyder and the new Emergency Financial Manager. Meanwhile, its mayor and city council have been forced to the sidelines. Self-rule, for the moment, is suspended for residents.

But this is only part of the challenge ahead for the city. The community still needs economic development, and the jobs this creates. The government is still faced with structural problems caused by a declining population, and the redistribution of wealth that has occurred. As for additional funding help, Detroit is at the mercy of a legislative majority that does not appear overly sympathetic. In addition, the city finds itself in a much weaker position in regard to any regional cooperative agreements with its suburban neighbors.

Adding to the difficulty has been the recent conviction of former Mayor Kwame Kilpatrick for running a criminal enterprise while in office. The verdict further fuels the negative perception that many people have about the city, and reinforces their inclination to ignore the city's plight. Along with all of these obstacles are the ever-present social problems of crime, alcohol and drug abuse, broken families, domestic violence, chronic unemployment, and high drop-out rates; problems that plague our entire society, but are magnified in the larger urban centers and hyped by the media. When all of this is put together, the challenge of turning things around for Detroit financially, socially, and economically, while at the same time allowing its residents some measure of control over their community, seems daunting.

"Hard stuff," Coleman Young might say.

But Young's story was one of perseverance, courage, and persistence… of standing your ground and holding firm to your beliefs. Of believing in yourself.

In the concluding paragraph, he evoked two images: One was of young, black men standing on the street corner and the other of the Presidents and captains of industry he had collaborated with during his 20 years as mayor. It was to the former, he said, that he felt allegiance… "Those brothers, slapping hands are young men out-of-luck, searching for human respect and a living wage."

Growing up in Detroit, he had been one of those young men. He never lost sight of that beginning, despite eventually rubbing elbows with the rich and powerful. A fair chance was all he asked for and what he did not always get growing up, but what he finally earned for himself, and what he wanted for his city and its residents. A fair chance is what all of us seek, and a fair chance is what we'll hopefully offer to Detroiters as they face this *hard stuff.*

The Long Crossing

The sign stands at the edge of the sidewalk, just west of the Holiday Inn parking lot, greeting passersby who are using this walkway that hugs the shoreline of the west arm of the bay. It's a historical marker, sporting the familiar gold lettering on a light green backdrop that reads:

GRAND TRAVERSE BAY

French traders named this bay when they made "the long crossing"— la grande traverse— across its mouth. Chippewa and Ottawa tribes dwelt in this region. Peter Dougherty's Indian Mission, established in 1839 at Old Mission, paved the way for white settlers. Founded in 1847, Traverse City was for years an important center of lumbering. Subsequently, it has become famous as the nation's cherry capital.

"That's it in a nutshell," you might say.

But this place is so much more for the thousands who reside here in northwestern Lower Michigan and for the thousands who visit the area, drawn here for all manner of reasons, not the least of which are the scenic vistas offered by this body of water and the hilly, wooded countryside that borders the shorelines.

During the brief time when I, too, called this place "home"— a span of about two years in the mid-1970s— I would walk each morning from the room I rented at the Whiting-Wares Hotel (for the princely sum of $25-a-week) to a restaurant called 'The Bean Pot' two blocks away. Both the hotel and the eatery were on Front Street, in the heart of the Downtown. Each offered a generous view of the bay. Drinking my coffee, I'd look out at the expanse of blue. In those first hours of a new day, it offered all sorts of different shades and hues, depending on the variation of sunlight and cloud cover. Those colors might range from gorgeous azure to ominous slate gray.

The restaurant was located beside the Boardman River at the corner of Front and Park Streets. The bridge that spanned this waterway connected the Downtown to the Grandview Parkway (that short, busy stretch of highway that allows motorists to by-pass the business district as they drive from one side of town to the other.) This route also provided an easy access to the beach at Clinch Park, located on the north side of the Parkway

Sometimes, after coffee, I'd walk over to the beach, sit at one of the benches, and enjoy the sound of the waves washing against the shore as well as the sight of the fishing boats scattered about. I'd tarry there for awhile, not quite ready on that particular day to return to my room and my ongoing attempts to rein in a mind teeming with unruly thoughts and ill-defined impressions; to harness this raw energy for the purpose of composing some insightful prose.

Now, on an August morning many years later, with wife and son back at the motel, I read the marker and then resume my stroll. No ghost of a younger self greets me on the route, only others who are also walking, or else jogging or riding a bike.

What have I become? I wonder that often as each day comes and goes, a successive pace not unlike the waves that lap the shore; a pace that seems to have quickened as I've reached and gone past my 60th year. And accompanying that thought, I wonder as well, "What is left?" The amount of time, yes, but more importantly what aspirations, hopes, and obtainments might still be within reach?

Will there be enough time? And, when all is said-and-done, will the reaching be worth the effort?

Later that day I wander about Horizon Books. The store is crowded. I pause next to a table where several of Jim Harrison's novels are on display. Harrison, who used to live in nearby Leelanau Peninsula, now resides in Montana. Posted on a wall next to these books is a note he sent to the owners, congratulating them on their 50th year in business, and remembering their kindness towards him when he was a young, unknown, and struggling writer.

I remember going frequently to their place of business when I lived here; only then it was located across the street, a little further to the west, and confined to a much smaller space. Still, then as now, it served as a beacon for those of us drawn to the printed word, a refuge where I could wile away an hour or two. I could not afford to buy much of their merchandise in those days. A book I did purchase was Harrison's *A Good Day to Die*, one of his first published works.

That evening we meet Randy and Buffy for dinner at North Peak, a former candy factory converted into a combination microbrewery and restaurant that's become a popular destination. We manage to secure a table before the line gets too long and, once seated we begin catching up with each others' lives since our previous visit. Over the years, whenever we drive up to this northern outpost for a quick vacation, I call them, and we arrange our dinner date.

I met Randy shortly after I arrived in Traverse City in May of 1974, shaking hands with him on that first evening when I began working as a cook at the Big Boy Restaurant. Back then the local franchise was located at Munson Avenue and Eighth Street. Randy was the supervisor for the night shift. I only lasted a few months as a line cook, while he stayed on for a couple of years. During that tenure he met his future wife who was a waitress on the day shift.

I attended their wedding. Afterwards I stayed in touch for a little while, contacting Randy when I came to town to do some fishing. But soon my trips stopped. And the seasons, as they say, came and went. Finally, one summer, now married myself, Dawn and I decided to spend one of our mini three-day vacations in Traverse City. ("My old stomping grounds when I was a wayward youth" was how I fondly characterized those days to friends and family.) While not sure what to expect, I decided to look Randy up on that visit and find out how he and Buffy were doing. It was one of my better ideas. Despite the passage of several years, we quickly picked up where we'd left off.

When I arrived here in the spring of 1974, it was on the eve of my sister Carol's death. She was only 21. My decision to come here was part reckless adventure, the kind of poorly-planned and questionable impulse that often guided my life. But this trip was also prompted by a realization that I had been drifting in an aimless manner, without any set purpose, dead in the water so to speak. I needed to do something—anything—to get going in a purposeful direction. In retrospect, I realize another motive existed, too; a rather ignoble one despite my trying to doll it up at the time. Coming here was an escape from what I instinctively, though unconsciously, knew was coming. I did not wish to watch my sister die.

After her funeral, I returned to Traverse City; my mother and her friend driving me back. They deposited me at the front door of the Whiting-Wares. I went back to work. The cooks and waitresses at the Big Boy served as a life-line in those ensuing weeks.

The day after I'd returned, I bought a rawhide shoelace. Tying it through my sister's class ring, I created a makeshift necklace. I waded out in the waters of the bay at Clinch Park that afternoon and put it around my neck, promising that "now I'll live for both of us, that I'll reach as high and as far as I could; that I'll make my life as special as I could."

"For both of us," I vowed.

But a few years later, back in my hometown of Fowlerville, not having done much of great note in either of those directions, not having gone too high or very far, and with nothing special to show for my efforts, I visited her gravesite. There I took off the necklace, and told her it was time for me to let her go… that living my own life was proving to be difficult enough. The time had come for me to accept her death, acknowledge the fact that she was irretrievably gone, and admit that there was nothing I could do, no way in which I could live my life that would alter this reality. The time had come for me to move on.

What have I become?

A husband, a father and grandfather, a friend, a newspaperman, and a writer. "That's it in a nutshell," you might say. But so much more. Those descriptive labels do not begin to convey the depth and breadth of my life story anymore than a marker next to a sidewalk can ever tell the history of this place.

La grande traverse... the long crossing. The journey will not, I hope, be over any time soon; still, I know, at least for me, a good portion of the distance has now been covered. A sunrise comes with each new day, there are tasks and routines to be pursued, and after the day's work is completed, a few lingering moments are left to savor as the sun sets and the shades of evening descend. This is "the petty pace" that Shakespeare lamented, but it's all we have; all we'll ever get. One more day. One more chance to greet life.

As I walk along the sidewalk beside Grand Traverse Bay on this summer morning, I look at the pale blue waters glimmering in the sun, and at the faraway line between blue water and blue sky that's barely discernible. I remember sitting at that makeshift desk, in front of the window in my room at the Whiting-Wares, enjoying a similar sight as I glanced up from the notepad; pausing in my effort to fashion my thoughts into something I felt would be meaningful... to write something that would reach high and far, that would be special... words that might touch others, and might last beyond my brief time here. A promise I made, and still try to keep; made long ago in the waters of this bay, to a sister gone, when the mornings were still fresh and life was still young, when the crossing stretched out, seemingly endless, beyond the far horizon.